LOTHIAN AND EDINBURGH ENTERPRISE LIMITED

FORTH PORTS PLC

LOTHIAN REGIONAL COUNCIL

CITY OF EDINBURGH DISTRICT COUNCIL

EDINBURGH TOURIST BOARD

*L*OOK WHO STEERED THE TALL SHIPS TO EDINBURGH.

*F*OR THE PAST THREE YEARS, five partners have worked together to make the 1995
Cutty Sark Tall Ships' Race and quayside events the best ever. We hope you're enjoying the results.

THIS SCHOONER HELPS YOUNG PEOPLE. WE'RE GLAD TO BE ON BOARD.

Every year hundreds of young people undergo training courses on the "Spirit of Scotland", a replica Victorian schooner operated by the Fairbridge Society. In partnership with Scottish Nuclear, this project is aimed at benefiting young people, and since the start of Scottish Nuclear's £1/2m sponsorship over 1000 young people have set sail on personal development training. Through learning new skills, young people can re-channel their energies in positive directions and make a constructive contribution to their community.

The Spirit of Scotland is taking part in this year's Tall Ships Race, and will be in Leith from 15-18 July. We're proud to say, we'll be with them all the way.

Scottish Nuclear

Scottish Nuclear Limited, 3 Redwood Crescent, Peel Park, East Kilbride, G74 5PR.

A STRONG LINK IN THE CHAIN OF LIFE.

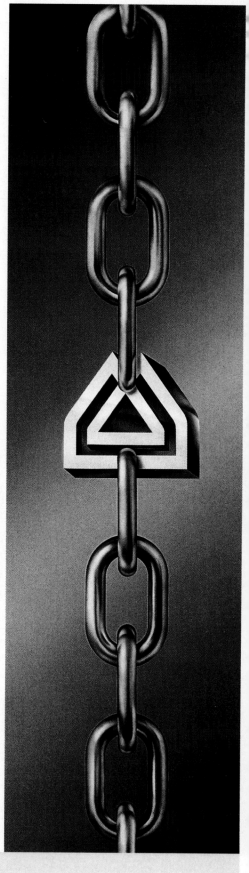

MILLER

UNIQUE CENTRE FOR TALL SHIPS ON THE TEES!

The proposals for the superb new sail training and tall ships repair facilities are now taking shape on the Tees.

Facilities at the Teesside National Tall Ships Centre will include covered halls and workshops, pontoons, a mobile marine hoist, a ship lift and transfer system and residential accommodation.

There will be a sail training and visitors centre and it will be possible for spectators to watch work going ahead from special high level walkways providing excellent viewing points across the dock.

The centre will utilise Teesside's traditional shipwright skills, which have already completed first class restoration work on two famous sail training ships, TS Royalist and the Sir Winston Churchill.

An announcement to build the largest sail training ship since 1905 in Great Britain has also been made by HRH The Princess Royal and Mr. Robin Knox-Johnston, Chairman of the Sail Training Association.

The Centre forms part of Teesside Development Corporation's redevelopment of Middlesbrough Dock, which includes large scale retail, commercial and leisure schemes.

The final piece of teak decking is put in place on TS Royalist by Sir Ronald Norman, Chairman of Teesside Development Corporation, watched by TDC's Chief Executive Duncan Hall and Captain Peter Grindal of the Sea Cadet Corps.

TEESSIDE NATIONAL Tall Ships CENTRE

The new Barquentine to be built on Teesside

Teesside National Tall Ships Centre will maintain and help train crews for these magnificent vessels into the next millennium.

The Teesside National Tall Ships Centre is a Flagship Scheme of

TEESSIDE
DEVELOPMENT CORPORATION

For further details contact Duncan Hall, Chief Executive, Teesside Development Corporation, Dunedin House, Riverside Quay, Stockton-on-Tees, Cleveland TS17 6BJ. Tel: (01642) 677123 Fax: (01642) 676123

See you in:

 Edinburgh
July 15 • July 18 • 1995

 Bremerhaven
July 23 • July 26 • 1995

 Frederikshavn
July 31 • August 3 • 1995

 Amsterdam
August 10 • August 14 • 1995

 Brugge/Zeebrugge
August 16 • August 20 • 1995

Follow the Tall Ships into the Future
*By the International
Sail Training Association's Race Director
Lt Col Peter J. Newell*

Such is the popularity of the Cutty Sark Tall Ships' Races that our plans are already fixed for the next five years. There is considerable competition to be selected as a host port for the race circuit, for example 18 different ports invited the fleet in 1998. The decision on which four ports will be successful in 1999 will be taken by the ISTA's International Racing Committee at our Annual International Conference in London in November. Sadly we cannot please everyone, but the races are generally allocated on an alternating four year cycle of areas to give each port a reasonable chance of being successful sooner or later!

1995
This year we are in the North Sea with the race starting from Edinburgh (Leith) in Scotland 15-18 July, 23-26 July in Bremerhaven (Germany) 31 July - 3August in Frederikshavn (Denmark) 10-14 August in Amsterdam (Holland). The Fleet will stay together after leaving Amsterdam to visit Zeebrugge (Belgium) 16-20 August.

1996
In 1996 we organise two races. First the Baltic race:

Rostock (Germany)	*06-09 July*
St Petersburg (Russia)	*18-21 July*
Turku (Finland)	*28-31 July*
Copenhagen (Denmark)	*7-10 August*

And the Mediterranean Race:

Genoa (Italy)	*13-16 July*
Palma Majorca (Spain)	*21-24 July*
Naples (Italy)	*31 July-3 August*

1997
In 1997 there will be a Northern orientation with a race from Aberdeen (Scotland) 12-15 July to Trondheim (Norway) 23-26 July. This is the furthest North the fleet will ever have been. From Trondheim the fleet will cruise in company to Stavanger (Norway) 3-6 August and then race from there to Gothenburg (Sweden) 13-16 August. Put this one in your diary now if you want to see the midnight sun and Trondheim's 1000th birthday party. Meantime in the Pacific, Sail Osaka

Mit den Tall Ships in die Zukunft
*von Lt. Col. Peter J. Newell, Regatta-Direktor
der „International Sail Training Association"*

Die Cutty-Sark Tall Ships' Races sind so beliebt, daß wir bereits für die nächsten fünf Jahre geplant haben. Dabei liegen die Gasthäfen in großem Wettstreit um für die Regattaserie ausgewählt zu werden, z.ß. haben 18 verschiedene Städte die Flotte für 1998 eingeladen. Die Entscheidung darüber, welche vier Häfen für 1999 gewählt werden, wird im November für vom Internationalen Regatta-Komitee der ISTA auf der Internationalen Jahreskonferenz in London getroffen. Leider können wir nicht allen Bewerbern gerecht werden, doch die Regatten werden üblicherweise in einem Vierjahreszyklus auf verschiedene Gebiete verteilt, damit jeder Hafen angemessene Gelegenheit zur früheren oder späteren Teilnahme erhält!

1995
In diesem Jahr treffen wir uns im schottischen Edinburgh/Leith (15. bis 18. Juli) und segeln dann über die Nordsee nach Bremerhaven (23. bis 26. Juli) und weiter nach Frederikshavn/Dänemark (31. Juli bis 3. August) und Amsterdam (10. bis 14. August). Nach dem Aufenthalt in Amsterdam bleibt die Flotte bis zur Ankunft im belgi-schen Zeebrugge (16. bis 20. August) zusammen.

1996
1996 veranstalten wir zwei Regatten, und zwar zuerst die Ostsee-Regatta:

Rostock (Deutschland)	*6. bis 9. Juli*
St. Petersburg (Rußland)	*18. bis 21. Juli*
Turku (Finnland)	*28. bis 31. Juli*
Kopenhagen (Dänemark)	*7. bis 10. August*

Und außerdem die Mittelmeer-Regatta:

Genua (Italien)	*13. bis 16. Juli*
Palma de Mallorca (Spanien)	*21.bis 24. Juli*
Neapel (Italien)	*31.Juli bis 3.Aug*

1997
1997 segeln wir zum ersten Mal in den höchsten Norden und veranstalten vom schottischen Aberdeen (12. bis 15. Juli) aus eine Regatta zum norwegischen Trondheim (23. bis 26. Juli), segeln dann in einer Gemeinschaftsfahrt nach Stavanger (ebenfalls Norwegen, 3. bis 6. August) und anschließend als Regatta zum schwedischen Göteborg (13. bis 16. August). Vermerken Sie diesen Termin gleich in Ihrem Kalender, wenn Sie die Tausendjahrfeier von Trondheim in der Mitternachtssonne erleben möchten. Gleichzeitig

Volg de Schepen in de Toekomst
(door de Raceleider van de International Sail Training Association Luit. Kol. Peter J. Newell)

De populariteit van de Cutty Sark Tall Ships **Races is zo groot dat onze plannen voor de** volgende vijf jaren al vast liggen. De concurrentie strijd om als gasthaven in het race-circuit te worden opgenomen is vrij groot. Zo hebben 18 verschillende havens de vloot uitgenodigd voor 1998. De beslissing welke vier havens in 1999 zullen worden aangedaan, zal tijdens onze Jaarlijkse Internationale Conferentie te Londen in november door ISTA's genomen worden. Helaas is het onmogelijk om het iedereen naar de zin te maken, maar de races worden in het algemeen toegewezen aan gebieden op een 4-jaar rotatiebasis, waardoor iedere haven vroeg of laat de kans krijgt!

1995
Dit jaar zijn we op de Noordzee, en de race zal starten in Edinburgh (Leith) in Schotland op 15-18 juli, 23-26 juli in Bremerhaven (Duitsland), 31 juli - 3 augustus in Frederikshavn (Denemarken), 10-14 augustus in Amsterdam (Nederland). De vloot zal daarna gezamelijk een bezoek brengen aan Zeebrugge (België) van 16-20 augustus.

1996
In 1996 worden er twee races georganiseerd. De eerste is de Baltische Race:

Rostock (Duitsland)	6- 9 juli
St. Petersburg (Rusland)	18-21 juli
Turku (Finland)	28-31 juli
Kopenhagen (Denemarken)	7-10 augustus

En de Middellandse Zee Race:

Genua (Italië)	13-16 juli
Palma Majorca (Spanje)	21-24 juli
Napels (Italië)	31 juli-3 aug

1997
In 1997 zal de aandacht op het Noorden gevestigd worden met een race van Aberdeen (Schotland), 12-15 juli, naar Trondheim (Noorwegen), 23-26 juli. Dit is het noordelijkste dat de race ooit geweest is. Van Trondheim zal de vloot gezamelijk naar Stavanger (Noorwegen), 3-6 augustus, zeilen waarna naar Gothenburg (Zweden), 13-16 augustus, geraced zal worden. Maak hiervan een aantekening in uw agenda als u de middernachtszon wil zien en de 1000ste vejaardag van Trondheim wil meemaken. Ondertussen zal Sail Osaka in de Pacific de

Publisher/Verlag/Uitgever
Anthony Churchill
Manager/Verlagsleiter/Manager
Guy Pearse
Production/Herstellung/Produktie
Cesar Rocha
Coordinator/Koordinator/Coordinator
Linda Miller
Printer/Druk/Drukker *Goodhead
Heatset, Bicester, Oxon, England.*
Reprohouse/Reprohaus/Reproductie
*Repro World, Thames House,
London E1, UK/Großbritannien/VK)*
© *Churbarry Enterprises Ltd.,
7 Craven Hill, London W2 3EN, UK
Tel: 0044(0)171 402 2247
Fax: 0044(0)171 402 1919.
Cover foto 'Kruzenshtern' by Beken
of Cowes.*

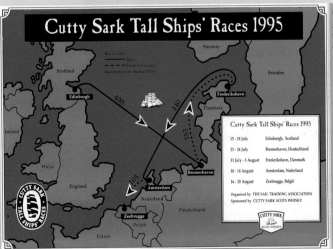

Cutty Sark Tall Ships' Races 1995

15 - 18 July	Edinburgh, Scotland
23 - 26 July	Bremerhaven, Deutschland
31 July - 3 August	Frederikshavn, Danmark
10 - 14 August	Amsterdam, Nederland
16 - 20 August	Zeebrugge, België

Organised by THE SAIL TRAINING ASSOCIATION
Sponsored by CUTTY SARK SCOTS WHISKY

Contents: First come general articles and articles on this year's ports. Then photos of major ships entered. Finally are lists of all participating ships with explanations of their rigs, their flags. **Most pages are in English, German, and Dutch.** *Der erste besteht aus allgemeinen Berichten und Artikeln zu den diesjährigen Häfen. Dann folgt ein Bildteil mit den wichtigen teilnehmenden Schiffen. Den Abschluß bilden Listen der gemeldeten Schiffe mit Erklärungen zu ihren Takelungsarten und Flaggen. **Den Mehrzahl der Seiten finden Sie in englisher, deutscher und hollandischer Sprache.*** In het eerste vindt men algemene nieuws, bijvoorbeld op de havens van dit jaar. Daarna komen photos van de betekendste schepen, en tenslotte lijsten van alle deelnemende schepen met inlichtingen op hun tuigage en vlaggen. **De pagina's zijn meestal in het Engels, Duits en Nederlands.**

International Yacht Restoration School

The IYRS is on the waterfront at Newport, Rhode Island, on the East Coast of the United States. Non profit making, it teaches students the skills, history and related sciences involved in the understanding, restoration and maintenance of classic sailing ships. It will collect, restore and preserve a fleet, maintain and use them for the purpose of teaching seamanship, navigation, sailing, boat handling and maintenance.

Small yachts of 40 ft or less will be restored, and the focus first will be the restoration of the last great American yacht, CORONET, pictured here. A 175 foot schooner built in 1885, she won the 1887 Transatlantic Race, made four round the world voyages via Cape Horn, and in Europe she visited Cowes, Gibraltar, Cherbourg, Toulon, Le Havre. From now, apprentices will be taken on, and students invited to the school. If you wish to become involved in any aspect of our work, please write to me, Elizabeth Meyer, c/o 7 Craven Hill, London W2 3EN, England.

commemorates the 100th Anniversary of the construction of the modern port of Osaka, with the course:

Hong Kong	26-29 March
Okinawa	11- 14 April
Kagoshima	20-22 April
Osaka	27 April- 5 May.

1998

In 1998 the ships return to the Western Approaches, from Falmouth (16-19 July) to Lisbon (31 July - 3 August), Vigo (9-12 August), and Dublin (22-25 August). There is also Tall Ships 1998 Australia, from Sydney to Hobart, and around Tasmania, starting 20th January.

1999

The ports have not been decided yet, but the intention is to race up the West Coast of the UK, around Scotland, and across the North Sea.

2000

'Tall Ships 2000 is busy planning a very special double trans-Atlantic race to celebrate the Millennium. This will take the form of a traditional clockwise circuit of the North Atlantic beginning in the UK and

feiert „Sail Osaka" im Pazifik das hundertjährigeJubiläum des modernen Hafens von Osaka mit folgender Route:

Hongkong	*26. bis 29. März*
Okinawa	*11. bis 14. April*
Kagoshima	*20. bis 22. April*
Osaka	*27. April bis 5. Mai*

1998

1998 kehren die Schiffe in den Westen zurück und segeln von Falmouth/Cornwall (16. bis 19. Juli) nach Lissabon (31. Juli bis 3. August), Vigo/Spanien (9. bis 12. August) und Dublin (22. bis 25. August). Außerdem findet in diesem Jahr vom 20. Januar an die Regatta „Tall Ships 1998 Australia" von Sydney nach Hobart und rund um Tasmanien statt.

1999

Die Entscheidung über die Auswahl der Häfen steht noch aus, doch planen wir eine Regatta entlang der Westküste von Großbritannien um Schottland herum und dann über die Nordsee.

2000

„Tall Ships 2000" plant anläßlich der Jahrtausendwende eine sehr ehrgeizige Doppelregatta über den Atlantik, wobei wir im März im traditionellen Uhrzeigersinn von Großbritannien und vom Mittelmeer starten und

100ste verjaardag van de bouw van Osaka's moderne haven herdenken, met de volgende route:

Hong Kong	26-29 maart
Okinawa	11-14 april
Kagoshima	20-22 april
Osaka	27 april - 5 mei.

1998

In 1998 keren de schepen terug naar het westen, van Falmouth (16-19 juli) naar Lisabon (31 juli - 3 augustus), Vigo (9-12 augustus) en Dublin (22-25 augustus). Er is verder ook nog een Tall Ships 1998 Australia, van Sydney naar Hobart, en rond Tasmanië, die op 20 januari van start gaat.

1999

Er is nog geen beslissing genomen over de havens, maar het is de bedoeling om langs de westkust van het Verenigde Koninkrijk, rond Schotland en over de Noordzee te racen.

2000

'Tall Ships 2000' is druk bezig met het plannen van een zeer speciale trans-atlantische race om de eeuwwisseling te vieren. Deze zal de vorm aannemen van een traditioneel circuit in de richting van de wijzers van de klok over de Atlantische Oceaan dat in het Verenigde Koninkrijk en in de Middellandse Zee in maart

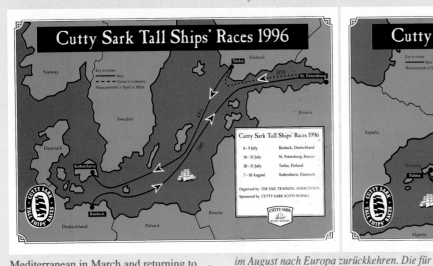

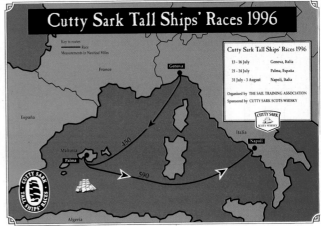

Mediterranean in March and returning to Europe in August. The ports for Tall Ships 2000 are Southampton (England) and Genoa (Italy) from where two separate fleets will race to Agadir (Morocco). From Agadir the combined fleet will race across the Atlantic to San Juan (Puerto Rico), After a cruise in Company calling at various US East Coast ports the fleet will be in New York for a grand Parade of Sail on the 4th of July. The fleet will then cruise up the cost to Halifax (Canada) from where the final race will be launched back across the Atlantic to Amsterdam (Holland).

If this year's races have whetted your appetite and you would like further details of future Cutty Sark Tall Ships' Races then write to me at:

The International Sail Training Association Race Office, *5 Mumby Road, Gosport, Hants PO12 1AA.*
Tel: 0044 (0) 1705 586367. Fax: 0044 (0) 1705 584661.

im August nach Europa zurückkehren. Die für die Veranstaltungen des Jahres 2000 ausgewählten Häfen sind Southampton/England und Genua/Italien, von wo zwei getrennte Regatten nach Agadir/Marokko stattfinden. Von dort aus geht die Regatta der vereinten Flotte weiter über den Atlantik nach San Juan/Puerto Rico. Nach Besuchen in verschiedenen Häfen der amerikanischen Ostküste trifft sich die Flotte zu einer großen Segelparade in New York am 4. Juli und kreuzt anschließend an der Küste entlang mit nördlichem Kurs nach Halifax/Kanada. Von dort startet die abschließende Regatta zurück über den Atlantik nach Amsterdam (Holland).

Wenn das Programm für dieses Jahr Ihr Interesse geweckt hat und Sie weitere Informationen zu den Cutty Sark Tall Ships' Races wünschen, schreiben Sie mir bitte unter folgender Anschrift.

The International Sail Training Association, Race Office, 5 Mumby Road, Gosport, Hants PO12 1AA, Großbritannien.
Tel: 0044(0) 1705 58 63 67 Fax: 0044(0) 1705 58 46 61

begint en in augustus naar Europa terugkeert. De havens die 'Tall Ships 2000' zal aandoen zijn Southampton (Engeland) en Genua (Italië) van waaruit twee aparte vloten naar Agadir (Maroco) zullen racen. Vanuit Agadir zal de gezamelijke vloot over de Atlantische Oceaan racen naar San Juan (Puerto Rico). Na een gezamelijke tocht naar verschillende havens aan de Amerikaanse oostkust zal de vloot New York aandoen voor een grootse zeilparade op 4 juli. De vloot zal dan verder langs de kust naar Halifax (Canada) zeilen waar de laatste race over de Atlantische Oceaan naar Amsterdam (Holland) van start zal gaan.

Als u tijdens de races van dit jaar de smaak te pakken hebt gekregen en meer wilt weten over toekomstige Cutty Sark Tall Ships' Races, schrijf dan naar het volgende adres:

The International Sail Training Association, Race Office, 5 Mumby Road, Gosport, Hants PO12 1AA. VK.
Tel: 0044(0) 1705 586367 Fax: 0044(0) 1705 584661.

CENTRE PAGES. THE START OF THE 1995 SERIES BEGINS WITH A PARADE OF SAIL.Just before the first bridge they turn and sail into the far distance where the Princess Royal starts the race.

(Im Mittelteil) Die Veranstaltungen 1995 beginnen mit einer Segelparade. Unmittelbar vor der ersten Brücke wenden die Schiffe und segeln hinaus, wo Ihre Königliche Hoheit die Prinzessin die Regatta startet.

(Middelste paginas). Die evenementen in 1995 beginnen met een zeilparade. Voor de eerste brug zullen ze wenden en zeilen naar het gebied, waar de Princess Royal de race zal starten.

Come along to the Cellnet Demonstration Units for exceptional mobile phone and accessory offers.

ATLAS

YOUR LOCAL SPECIALIST WITH NATIONWIDE BT SUPPORT

Branches at:

GLASGOW
0141 557 0707

DUMFRIES
01387 255255

CARLISLE
01228 595151

AYR
01292 280000

Communications Centre

The purchase of a mobile phone is subject to connection to a Cellnet tariff with a BT Mobile communications airtime agreement. Subject to status and availability. Offer only available 15-18 July 1995 at the Tall Ships Race, Port of Leith, Edinburgh.

In the annual Cutty Sark Tall Ships' Races, attention is naturally concentrated on the ships and on the young people forming the crews. These are the people who benefit most from the experience, but that should not obscure the vitally important work of the International Sail Training Association in organising the races; the support of the race sponsor 'Cutty Sark', and the generous hospitality of the host ports.

In 1995 the Tall Ships gather in Edinburgh and then the fleet races across the North Sea to Bremerhaven and on to Frederikshavn, Amsterdam, and Zeebrugge. All these ports are making great efforts to offer a warm welcome to the young crews. Their contribution is vital to the success of the whole project.

Bei den alljährlichen „Cutty Sark Tall Ships' Races" stehen selbstverständlich die Schiffe und ihre jungen Mannschaften im Mittelpunkt des Interesses. Diese jungen Leute sammeln überaus reiche Erfahrungen, doch sollten darüber nicht die unverzichtbare Organisationstätigkeit der International Sail Training Association, die Unterstüzung der Regatta-Sponsoren von „Cutty Sark" und die großzügige Gastfreundschaft der Häfen vergessen werden.

1995 treffen sich die teilnehmenden Hochseeschiffe in Edinburgh, und von dort segelt die Flotte über die Nordsee nach Bremerhaven und weiter nach Frederikshavn, Amsterdam und Zeebrugge. Alle diese Häfen sind umfassend darauf vorbereitet, diese jungen Mannschaften herzlich willkommen zu heißen. Ihr Beitrag zu dieser Veranstaltung ist von entscheidender Bedeutung für den Erfolg des gesamten Projekts.

Tijdens de jaarlijkse Cutty Sark Tall Ships' Races, gaat de aandacht natuurlijk voornamelijk uit naar de schepen en de jonge mensen die de bemanning vormen. Dit zijn de mensen die het meest profiteren van deze ervaring, maar hierdoor moeten we niet het uiterst belangrijke werk van de International Sail Training Association vergeten die deze races organiseert; de steun van de race sponsor 'Cutty Sark', en de hartelijke gastvrijheid van de gast havens.

In 1995 verzamelen de Tall Ships in Edinburgh waarna de vloot over de Noordzee naar Bremerhaven zal racen en verder naar Frederikshavn, Amsterdam en Zeebrugge. Al deze havens doen enorme moeite om een warm welkom te bieden aan de jonge bemanningen. Hun bijdrage is van essentieel belang voor het succes van het hele project.

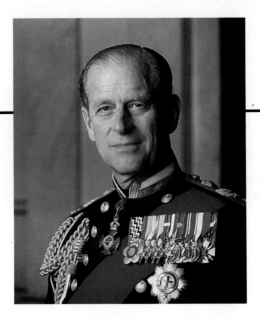

SAINT-

The Magic Port of Call

Past the Môle des Noires breakwater lined up with the cathedral spire, the port-city of Saint-Malo opens its gates to the Cutty Sark Tall ships.

Saint-Malo, the «Corsair City» that built it reputation and fame on th bravery and exploits of its glorious seamen, hoisted a colours for the finale of th '94 edition of the Cutty Sark Tall Ships' Race, to welcome the most prestigious armada of tall ships in the world.

After locking into the inner docks, at walking distance to the city, the fleet f a summer week or so revived the real picture of earlier Sain Malo, when the City was harbouring Eastern Indian C clippers and Newfoundlander cod fishing ships.

That was a magic moment; for everyone ...

Hundreds of thousands of visitors came to admire the round sterns or flared bows, o pace the teak gangways of the four-masted square riggers; international crews, young trainees and seasoned sailors alike, all enjoyed and appreciated the welcome granted by the keen people of Saint-Malo.

The «Malouins» are proud or the history which

Information
Direction Municipale des Sports, Fax. (33) 99.56.63.76
Office de Tourisme, Bassin des Yachts, 35400 Saint-Malo, France, Tél. (33)99.56.64.48, Fax. (33) 99.40.93.13
Photos Philip Plisson / Office de Tourisme, Michel Dupuis / Mairie de Saint-Malo.

Windward

MALO

ade their city a privileged
rt of call. Not only for the
ography and ergonomics of
e port, but also for the
aracter of the inhabitants,
o accord their living to the
ythm of the tides ...

To share the last tot
th the crews was not only a
ivilege, but also a welcome
ity...

e City en fête

Flags, bunting, shop
ndows and cafes, all the city
d turned golden.. the clamor
street bands, the beach
urnaments, the crew's
rade, as well as the more
rmal receptions and diners,
e cheerful and highly
notional prize giving
remony in the castle yard, all
ntributed to making that
ish call an unforgettable
oment.

Watching the onlookers'
ces when those halyard
ocks and capstans were
ueaking under the strain left
doubt as to their emotions..
This communion of the
ublic with some two thousand
ung trainees made another
apter of Saint-Malo's history.

Crowds under spell along the walls and Privateers' Mansions

Tall ships love Saint-
Malo : Belem, the STA
Schooners, Eendracht, and a
few others are regular callers;
Amerigo Vespucci is expected
for an official visit nest August,
as a token of Italian Navy's
gratitude for last years'
welcome to Corsario and Stella
Polare...

Tall ships and the Cutty
Sark Tall Ships' Races will not
be absent from this year's local
election agenda ; Malouins are
determined to include the
CSTSR in their heritage,
besides the prestigious «Route
du Rhum».

For us, the 1994 finish
was a good start. Speaking of a
good start.....1999 ?

Hundreds of ships and boats carrying all colours

Saint-Malo, a historic finish

CUTTY SARK TALL SHIPS RACE PORT OF LEITH EDINBURGH 1995

The Partnership behind the visit of the 1995 Cutty Sark Tall Ships' Race to the Port of Leith, Edinburgh would like to offer its grateful thanks to the following companies for their generous support

Official sponsors

300 YEARS OF BANKING SERVICE

SCOTTISH BREWERS

Sponsors

EAST COAST

BP

✚ **British Red Cross**
Edinburgh Branch
Caring for people in crisis

MARKS & SPENCER

Scottish Nuclear

Associate

THE GREAT OUTDOOR SPECIALIST

BAILLIE GIFFORD & Co

Supporters

CHANCELOT MILLS LTD	CANVAS HOLIDAYS	CARLTON HIGHLAND HOTEL	LEITH MILLS
D AND B CATERING (SCOTLAND) LTD	JEWEL AND ESK VALLEY COLLEGE	HARRY RAMSDEN'S	KELLY'S COPIERS
LAIMAR ENGINEERING LTD	QUEEN MARGARET COLLEGE	RRS DISCOVERY	THE VINTNERS ROOMS

Cutty Sark Tall Ships' Race 1995 - Port of Leith, Edinburgh
15th - 18th July
Project Director: John Ling   Project Officer: Fiona McGovern   Sponsorship Manager: David Copeland
Business Opportunities Manager: Graham Sinclair   Public Events Manager: Charlie Mussett
Site Services & Operations Manager: Roger Krys   PR & Media Manager: Libby Elles

Cutty Sark Tall Ships' Races are organised by the Sail Training Association and sponsored by Cutty Sark Scots Whisky

CUTTY SARK TALL SHIPS RACE BROUGHT TO YOU BY

EDINBURGH TOURIST BOARD

FORTH PORTS PLC

LOTHIAN REGIONAL COUNCIL

EDINBURGH THE CITY OF EDINBURGH DISTRICT COUNCIL

Lothian and Edinburgh Enterprise Limited

CUTTY SARK TALL SHIPS' RACES

EDINBURGH, *Port of Leith*

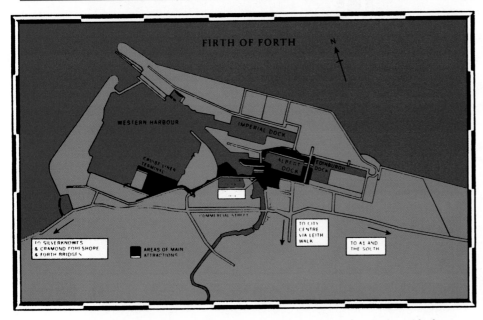

Above and below: the Port of Leith, showing where the ships will be moored, alongside the areas of Main Attraction. Photo: Copyright reserved: The Royal Commission on the Ancient and Historical Monuments of Scotland.

The Port of Leith is Edinburgh's maritime gateway to Europe and the world beyond. It began as the small settlement of South Leith at the mouth of the Water of Leith that runs down through Edinburgh to the Firth of Forth. In the time of David I of Scotland (1124-1153) it gained prominence, and by the 16th Century it was Scotland's chief port, even though it still lay within the mouth of a small river. The position was one of power rather than size in those feudal times.

The modern port began to take shape in the late 18th Century as dry docks and quays began to build out into the Firth, protected from the tidal waters by locks. Commercial shipping began. The first steamship was built in 1837, and the last sailing ship launched in 1932. In between, the port built huge vessels like Kobenhavn, a five masted barque. Today, shipbuilding has gone, but the port thrives under the ownership of Forth Ports PLC.

The town of Leith

Leith has been the centre of great events in Scotland's history, and has seen the landing of many monarchs in its time. Mary Queen of Scots returned to her native land from France at Leith in 1561, beginning the saga of the Jacobite claim to the united crown. But in 1822, when King George IV landed at Leith to begin a visit to Scotland all those issues had been resolved. In between, and to follow those great events Leith grew from a village into a town.

For a short period it even achieved independence from Edinburgh, and was the site of the world's first recorded golf club, and the members played on Leith Links, only a hundred yards or so from the port. Those Links will be the scene of Leith's Festival on the Saturday and Sunday of the Tall Ships visit, and they will be the terminus of the Leith pageant on Sunday after its floats and bands have entertained the crowds down Leith Walk and other streets in Leith.

See the Tall Ships in Leith.

All the ships in the Cutty Sark Tall Ships' Race fleet are berthed either in the Albert Dock and the neighbouring Prince of Wales Dock, or at the Cruise Liner Terminal. These areas, with a huge programme of entertainment, are open to the public from 10 o'clock every morning from Saturday 15th to Monday 17th July. They will close at 10 o'clock at night, except for Monday when they will open for much longer to enable everyone to see the fabulous Bank of Scotland tercentenary fireworks display.

Take the Park and Ride

Traffic can be a real problem with hundreds of thousands of people every day coming down to the quays. Use the organisation that will deliver you right into the heart of the Cutty Sark

**THE CUTTY SARK
TALL SHIPS' RACE
1997**

'Northern Light'
Aberdeen to Trondheim,
Stavanger to Göteborg
12 July - 16 August 1997

*The ports of Aberdeen, Trondheim, Stavanger and Göteborg invite you to join us for the
1997 Cutty Sark Tall Ships' Race. We promise you an international celebration of friendship and adventure
in the breathtaking beauty of Scotland and Scandinavia.*

Further information can be obtained from:

John Ling Aberdeen tel: +44 1224 648666   **Astrid Bjørgen** Trondheim tel: +47 73 52 80 15

Jostein Haukali Stavanger tel: +47 51 50 86 16   **Leif Aronsson** Göteborg tel: +46 31 81 82 01

Leith's refurbished riverfront, with exciting new bars and restaurants, hotel and history. Photo Edinburgh Tourist Office.

Tall Ships' Race area. Whatever road you take to Edinburgh you'll find Park and Ride signs which will deliver you to a free car park, and then it will deliver you to the berthing areas for a modest return trip fare (mostly £1.00, £1.50 from the Gyle, or 50p near Leith). Entry to the Dock is free; and when ships open to the public (it's up to them when they do) this is free as well. Take the strain out of the journey for you and your family, and leave the worries of your car behind you.

CUTTY SARK TALL SHIPS' RACE

LISBON SAIL - 98

On the 500th anniversary of the arrival of Vasco da Gama in India and the opening of a new age of maritime routes, the City of Lisbon, the Lisbon Port Authority, the National Committee for the Commemorations of Portugese Discoveries, the EXPO '98 - LISBON and APORVELA are welcoming the Tall Ships taking part in LISBON SAIL - 98, during their visit from 31st July to 3rd August, 1998.

VASCO DA GAMA MEMORIAL

DESPORTO

Porto de Lisboa

EXPO'98

APORVELA

THE OFFICIAL SWEATSHIRT FOR 1995. Extra Large (XL) or Large (L).Please send me ....XL and .... L.

DAS OFFIZIELLE SWEATSHIRT für die veranstaltung.
Extra groß (XL), oder Groß (L).
Bestellformular: Bitte Schicken sie mir....XL.........L

HET OFFICIELE RACE SWEATSHIRT
Extra Large(XL) of Large(L).
Bestelformulier: Stuur mij
a.u.b.....XL...........L

@£47.00/*120DM*/480DKK/132Hfl/2400BF.

Cheques to/*sheck an*/cheques betaalbaar aan Churbarry Enterprises Ltd, 7 Craven Hill, London W2 3EN, England.

My name/*Mein Name*/Mijn Naam................................
My address/*Meine Anschrift*/Mijn Adres....................................

....

....

....

Cutty Sark
Tall Ships' Race
Frederikshavn
31. juli - 3. august 1995

FREDERIKSHAVN

We are proud to welcome the Cutty Sark Tall Ships to our port for the third time. The first time was in 1980, then in 1984, and now in 1995. We're planning some superb entertainments in the harbour and in the town. The Tall Ships arrive on the 30th and 31st of July. On the 30th is the official opening, with mini tattoo by military orchestras, followed by a concert. Then on the 31st there is folk dancing, a captain's reception, and a jazz concert. On the 1st, a squaredancing display, sports competitions for the crew, the crews' parade and prize giving to the winners of the sports competition, followed by the crews party. On the 2nd, more sports, a sailing race for the handicapped, the captains' briefing and dinner, a historical festival play and march through the town centre, a recreation of a 17th Century battle (Norwegian/Danish soldiers against the Swedes), followed by

a night time lasershow. Daily, there are concerts in the tent, (no fee), swimming, sighteeing, special exhibitions, circus and theatre for children, helicopter sightseeing (you need tickets), and displays by rescue services, parachutists, and balloons ascents. During this period, the Province is to have a scratch lottery, and the funds go to youth work in a number of towns. On the 3rd, all too soon, the fleet departs. We hope you will enjoy your stay.

Vi er stolte over at byde Cutty Sark Tall Ships velkommen for tredje gang. Første gang var i 1980, derefter i 1984 og nu i 1995. Vi har planlagt et righoldigt underholdningsprogram på havnen or i byen. Skibene ankommer den 30. og 31. juli. Den 30. juli finder den officielle åbning sted; med mini tattoo fremført af militærorkestre - efterfulgt af en koncert i festteltet på havnen.
Den 31. juli er der et stort nordisk folkedansertræf, en reception for skibenes kaptajner samt en jazz koncert. I. august fort-

sætter programmet med opvisning af squaredans, sportskonkurrencer for besætningsmedlemmer, foruden overækkelse af sportspræmier. Om aftenen holdes fest for alle besætningsmedlemmerne. Sportsaktiviteterne for besætningerne fortsætter den 2. august, bl.a. kan nævnes en kapsejlads for handikappede. For kaptajnerne er der briefing om sejladsen til Amsterdam samt midday og om aftenen er der et stort historisk festspil ved Nordre Skanse, hvor Tordenskjolds soldater forsvarer sig mod svenskerne. Dagen slutter med et lasershow ud over hele havnen.
Desuden er der hver dag koncerter i festteltet (fri entre), special udstillinger, børnecirkus og - teater, helikopterterflyvning (billetter), opvisning med Falcks Redningskorps, faldskærmudspring og ballon-opstigninger.
Frem til og med den 2. august kan der købes skrabelodder med mange store præmier. Overskuddet går til ungdomsforeninger. Alt for tidligt, den 3. august, forlader skibene havnen. Vihåber alle vil nyde opholdet her i byen.

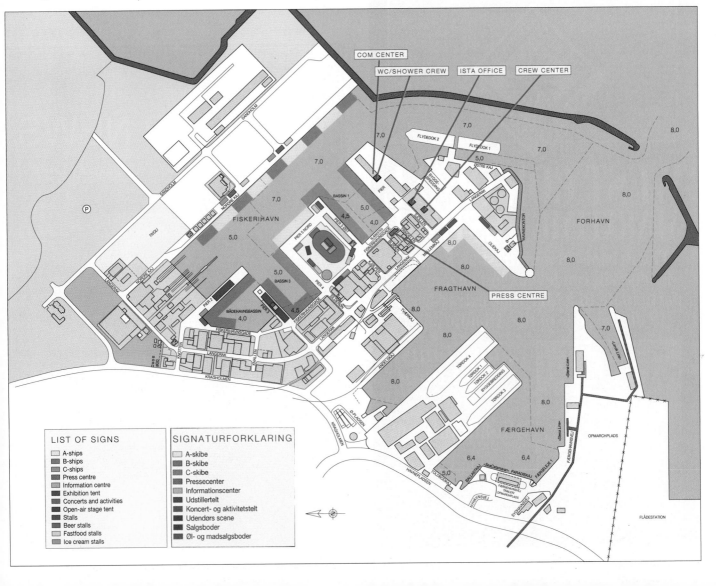

LIST OF SIGNS
- A-ships
- B-ships
- C-ships
- Press centre
- Information centre
- Exhibition tent
- Concerts and activities
- Open-air stage tent
- Stalls
- Beer stalls
- Fastfood stalls
- Ice cream stalls

SIGNATURFORKLARING
- A-skibe
- B-skibe
- C-skibe
- Pressecenter
- Informationscenter
- Udstillertelt
- Koncert- og aktivitetstelt
- Udendors scene
- Salgsboder
- Øl- og madsalgsboder

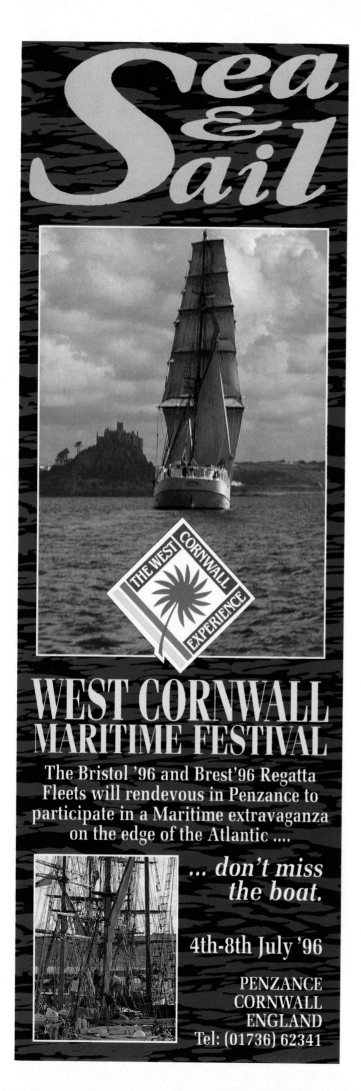

BREMERHAVEN

The seaside City of Bremerhaven is going to be a meeting place of an international sailing fleet of more than 20 nations again from July 21 to 26. As its patron, the President of the Federal Republic, Roman Herzog, will take the salute of the parade of all large and small windjammers ranging from small sloops to four masted barques, on the River Weser.

For the International Festival of the Windjammer 'Sail Bremerhaven '95', it is intended to present a comprehensive schedule of events including the following major attractions.

July 15-20. "Spezialisten", a meeting of a fleet of specialist vessels during the 21st Bremerhaven Festival with its Maritime Bazaar.

July 21-26 "Sail Bremerhaven '95" - the International Festival of the Windjammer, with the Cutty Sark Tall Ships' Race, July 23-26.

July 21-26 The Summer Meeting of Friends of the Gaff Rig.

Nach den großen Erfolgen von "Sail Bremerhaven 86", "Windjammer 90" und "Columbus 92" ist die Seestadt Bremerhaven vom 21.-26. Juli wieder Treffpunkt einer internationalen Seglerflotte aus über 20 Nationen. Budespräsident Roman Herzog wird als Schirmherr die Parade der großen und kleinen Windjammer von der Sloop bis zur Viermast-Bark auf der Weser abnehmen.

Zum internationalen Festival der Windjammer "Sail Bremerhaven '95" wird ein umfangreiches Programm vorgestellt, das folgende Hauptelmente hat:

15.-20. Juli. "Spezialisten", das Flottentreffen der Spezialschiffe zur internationalen 21. Bremerhaven Festwoche mit Basar Maritim.

21.-26. Juli. "Sail Bremerhaven '95", das Internationale Festival der Windjammer mit dem Cutty Sark Tall Ships' Race vom 23.-26. Juli.

21.-26. Juli. Das Soomertreffen der Freunde das Gaffelriggs.

KAISERFEN
Liegeplätze für die Schiffe der Klasse A,B,C
(beide Kajenseiten)
Berthing Classes A,B,C (Both pier sides).

NEUER HAFEN
Liegeplätze für die Schiffe der Klasse A,B
(beide Kajenseiten), Klasse C (Westseite)
Berthing Class A,B (Both pier sides),
Class C (Western side)

"KRUZENSHTERN"

ALTER HAFEN
Berthing Class C
Liegeplätze für die Schiffe der Klasse C

Liegeplätze für/Berthing "BOA ESPERANCA"
Portuguese Exhibition/Portugal-Ausstellung-
"Portugals Öffnung der Welt"

Berthing Class C
Liegeplätze für die Schiffe der Klasse C

Bank of Scotland Tercentenary Fireworks 17th July 1995

OFFICIAL BANKERS
to the Edinburgh Visit of the Cutty Sark
TALL SHIPS RACE 1995
PORT OF LEITH

CUTTY SARK
TALL SHIPS RACE
PORT OF LEITH
EDINBURGH
1995

BANK OF SCOTLAND
A FRIEND FOR LIFE

AMSTERDAM

Amsterdam is proud to welcome the Cutty Sark Tall Ships' Race as part of the fifth 'Sail Amsterdam Festival'. Their 100 or so Tall Ships will be joined by at least 800 other boats, from classic yachts, steam tugs, Chinese Dragon boats, rowing boats, wherries and scows plus traditional Dutch, English, Chinese, Irish and other racing, fishing and trading vessels.

Of special interest will be some rare replicas.

For instance the two Dutch East Indiamen AMSTERDAM and BATAVIA who will take part in the Parade of SAIL at the start of the Festival. Both will be open to the public throughout.

A German 13th Century trading vessel UBENA VON BREMEN, will be there, and BOA ESPERANÇA identical to the ships the Portugese used in their famous Voyages of Discovery to India, 500 years ago, before Columbus.

A "chayka", called "Presvyata Pohrova" - LADY OF SHELTER, will be there from the Ukraine as a replica of a 3rd Century Cossack warship.

In addition 70 classic vessels - including Thames barges - will race from Lowestoft and will arrive in IJmuiden on August 8th, to take part in the Festival.

Festivities will centre on the IJ harbour, and the famous Amsterdam canals will also be alive with races, parades, carnivals, competitions and displays.

On the 10th of August the highlight is the Parade of SAIL from IJmuiden. Tall ships accompanied by the Dutch traditional fleet will sail to Amsterdam where they arrive around noon.

On the 11th events include KPN Dragon Boat Races, the Nissan Aqua Flower Parade with steam tugs covered with flowers, and the Royal Netherlands Navy demonstration on land, water, and in the air.

On the 12th, the Postbank Canaltour includes historical motorboats, and the Heineken Pieremachocheltour is a tour of the canals of Amsterdam with everything that floats.

On the 13th, in the afternoon, is a fleet review on the IJ river. On the 14th, unfortunately this is the last day, with all the ships, including the Tall Ships, leaving the IJ harbour through the North Sea Canal on their way to the docks in IJmuiden.

Amsterdam is trots de Cutty Sark Tall Ships' Race te mogen verwelkomen als onderdeel van het vijfde SAIL Amsterdam evenement. Circa 100 Tall Ships zullen vergezeld worden door een vloot van tenminste 800 andere schepen, bestaande uit klassieke jachten, stoomsleepboten, Chinese Drakenboten, roeisloepen, wherry's en natuurlijk de traditionele Nederlandse, Engelse, Chinese, Ierse en andere wedstrijd-vissers-en handelsschepen. Speciale aandacht zal uitgaan naar een aantal zeldzame replica's, zoals bijvoorbeeld de twee VOC-schepen AMSTERDAM en BATAVIA die beiden mee zullen varen in de Parade of SAIL "In" op de eerste dag van SAIL 95 Amsterdam. Beide schepen zijn gedurende SAIL 95 Amsterdam's ochtends toegankelijk voor het publiek.

Andere replica's zullen zijn, het 13e eeuwse Duitse koggeschip UBENA VON BREMEN en het Portugese karveel BOA ESPERANÇA dat identiek is aan de schepen die de Portugezen 500 jaar geleden, vóór Columbus, gebruikten voor hun ontdekkingsreizen naar India. De Ukraïnse Chayka, LADY OF SHELTER genaamd, is een 3e eeuws Kozakken schip die zij gebruikten voor oorlogvoering.

70 klassieke schepen, inclusief de Thames barken zullen van Lowestoft naar IJmuiden racen, alwaar zij op 8 augustus zullen finishen om deel te kunnen nemen aan de festiviteiten van SAIL 95 Amsterdam.

Het festijn vindt plaats in de IJhaven en de beroemde Amsterdamse grachten waar races, tochten en demonstraties zullen plaatsvinden.

Op 10 augustus zal de Parade of SAIL van IJmuiden naar Amsterdam het hoogtepunt vormen. De Tall Ships zullen, vergezeld door de Nederlandse traditonele vloot van rondeen platbodemschepen naar Amsterdam varen, waar zij rond 12.00 uur aankomen.

Op 11 augustus zullen de KPN Drakenbootraces en de demonstraties van de Koninklijke Marine ter land, ter zee en in de lucht plaatsvinden. Het Nissan Aquacorso laat stoomsleepboten, versierd met prachtige bloemcomposities zien.

Op 12 augustus staan onder andere de Postbank Grachtentocht en de Heineken Pierernachocheltocht, waarbij alles wat drijft zal deelnemen, op het programma. De tochten zullen door de Amsterdamse grachten voeren.

Op zondag middag 13 augustus neemt de admiraal de vlootschouw af op het IJ.

De laatste dag, 14 augustus zal de gehele vloot, inclusief alle Tall Ships, van SAIL 95 Amsterdam vertrekken in de Parade of SAIL "out" richting IJmuiden.

Honderden deelnemende traditionele Nederlandse schepen in verschillende klassen. Sommigen met zijzwaarden en anderen zonder.
Hundreds of traditional Dutch ships take part, in different classes, some with 'leeboards' and some without.
(2 photoes).

Replica van de AMSTERDAM, een 17e eeuws VOC-schip
Replica of the AMSTERDAM, a 17th Century trading vessel with the East Indies and India.

ZEEBRUGGE

In 1995 the Brugge-Zeebrugge Port Authority (MBZ) is celebrating its 100th Anniversary, with the third visit of Tall Ships to Zeebrugge (16th to 20th August), after 1985's Royal Inauguration of the new port, and the 1990 visit. On 19th there is a Grand Parade of ships and boats from the centre of Brugge to Zeebrugge, followed by fireworks. Then on the 20th a final Parade of the Tall Ships ends the years events.

En 1995, les Autorités Portuaires de Bruges-Zeebrugge (MBZ) célébrent leur centenaire. Ce centenaire sera commémoré comme it se doit par une célébration prestigieuse couronné par le séjour des grand voiliers qui participent au Cutty Sark Tall Ships' Race et par la Grande Parade Bruges-Zeebrugge 1995. Les voiliers seront amarrés dans l'arrière-port de Zeebrugge du 16 au 20 août.

In 1995 viert het Havenbestuur Brugge-Zeebrugge (MBZ) zijn honderjarig bestaan Dit eeuwfeest zal passend herdacht worden met een grootse viering, waarvan het verblijf van de grote zeilschepen die deelnemen aan de Cutty Sark Tall Ships' Race en de Grote Parade Brugge ZB'95 de blikvangers zullen zijn. De zeilschepen zullen verblijven in de achterhaven van Zeebrugge van 16 tot 20 augustus.

A Western breakwater/*Jetée Ouest*/Westelijke dam
B Wielingen Dock/*Bassin Wielingen*/Wienlingendok
C Eastern breakwater/*Jetée est*/Oostelijke dam
D Container Dock/*Bassin Albert II*/Albert II-dok
E Brittannia Dock/*Brittanniadock* /Brittanniadok
F Pierre Vandammelock/*Ecluse PV*/ Pieer Vandammesluis
G Connection Basin/*Darse de jonction*/Verbindingsdok
H Northern Dock/*Bassin nord*/Noordelijk insteeldok
I Southern Dock/*Basin sud*/Zuidelijlk Insteekdok
J Visart Lock/*Ecluse Visart*/Visartsluis

Ships are moored in areas G (East), H, and I (24/East). *Les bateaux sont amarrés dans les zones G(est), H et I (24/est).* De schepen leggen aan in zones G (oost),H en I (24)(oost).

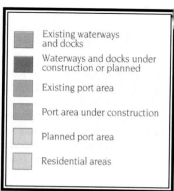

	Existing waterways and docks
	Waterways and docks under construction or planned
	Existing port area
	Port area under construction
	Planned port area
	Residential areas

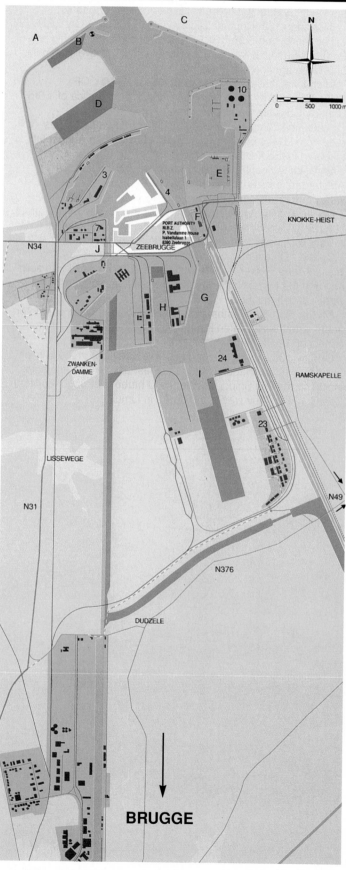

BOA ESPERANÇA (Portugal)

She's in Bremerhaven, Amsterdam and Zeebrugge only, a replica of Portugal's pioneering ships which 500 years ago sailed south around Africa to India, before Columbus sailed west to America. She uses a lateen rig.

Diese Replika der portugiesischen Pionierschiffe, die vor 500 Jahren auf dem Weg nach Indien Afrika im Süden rundeten, bevor Kolumbus gen Westen nach Amerika segelte, trägt ein Lateinerrigg. Sie wird nur in Bremerhaven, Amsterdam und Zeebrügge dabeisein.

Alleen maar in Bremerhaven, Amsterdam en Zeebrugge te zien en de latiengetuigde replica van de portugese schepen, die 500 jaren geleden rond Afrika de zuidelijke zeeweg naar Indie pioneerden voor Columbus naar Amerika zeilde. Foto: Beken of Cowes

SAGRES (Portugal/*Portugal*/Portugal)

Built in 1937 in Germany, she transfered to the USA, to Brazil, and finally Portugal. She is named after the place in Southern Portugal where Prince Henry the Navigator pioneered modern navigation methods, more than 500 years ago.

Dieses Schiff wurde einst im Jahre 1937 in Deutschland gebaut und gelangte über die USA und Brasilien schließlich nach Portugal. Es ist nach jenem Ort benannt, wo Heinrich der Seefahrer vor 500 Jahren die modernen Navigationsverfahren entwickelte.

Gebouwd in 1937 in Duitsland en overgedaan aan de Verenigde Staten, aan Brazilië en uiteindelijk aan Portugal. Ze is genoemd naar de plaats in Zuid-Portugal waar Prins Hendrik de Navigator meer dan 500 jaren geleden moderne navigatiemethoden gepionierd heeft.

OOSTERSCHELDE

(Netherlands/*Niederlande*/Nederland)

From 1917 she was a freighter in the Mediterranean and along Africa's coast. Now she is the Netherlands' largest restored sailing ship.

Dieses Schiff wurde von 1917 an als Frachtschiff im Mittelmeer und entlang der afrikanischen Küste eingesetzt und ist heute das größte restaurierte Segelschiff der Niederlande.

Een vrachtvaarder vanaf 1917 in de Middellandse Zee en langs de kust van Afrika. Nu het grootste gerestaureerde Nederlandse zeilschip.

CHRISTIAN RADICH

(Norway/*Norwegen*/Noorwegen)

Built in 1937 she was taken to Germany in 1940 where she capsized. In 1945 she was found and refloated, and later she resumed her three monthly training cruises.

Dieses 1937 gebaute Schiff wurde 1940 nach Deutschland gebracht, wo es kenterte. 1945 wurde es gehoben und nahm später seine dreimonatigen Schulkreuzfahrten wieder auf.

Dit schip werd gebouwd in 1937 en in 1940 naar Duitsland afgevoerd, waar ze kapseisde. Ze werd in 1945 teruggevonden en naar boven gehaald en hervatte later haar drie maand lange opleidingstochten. Foto: Beken of Cowes.

STELLA POLARE (Italy/*Italien*/Italië)

Italy's representative is a fine ship, maybe the fastest in the fleet. Owned by the Italian Navy, she carries the splendid Italian Navy's coat-of-arms on her spinnaker. Here she is in a previous race, speeding ahead.

Stellvertreter Italiens ist ein schönes Schiff, vielleicht das schnellste der Flotte. Es gehört der italienischen Marine und führt ihr prächtiges Wappen auf dem Spinnaker. Hier ist sie in einem der früheren Rennen zu sehen.

Italie woordt gerepresenteerd door een fijn schip, misschien het snelste van de vloot. Ze is eigendom van de Italiaanse Marine en zal haar prachtig wapen op de spinnaker laten zien. Hier zeilt ze in een eerder race. Photo: Beken of Cowes.

THISTLE (UK/*Großbritannien*/VK)

She is the only Thames Barge in this race, built for trading especially over the shallow mudbanks that surround the River Thames and England's East Coast. Thistle is unique, the only such barge to be built in Scotland - hence her name after Scotland's emblem. Thames Barges are also gathering at Amsterdam.

In dieser Regatta ist sie das einzige Plattbodenschiff von der Themse, speziell gebaut für die Frachtfahrt über die flachen Schlickbänke im Fluß und an Englands Ostküste. "Thistle" ist auch die einzige dieses Schiffstyps, die in Schottland gebaut wurde - sie wurde nach Schottlands Symbol, der Distel, benannt. Themse-Schiffe treffen sich auch in Amsterdam.

In de race is ze de enkele Thames Barge, gebouwd voor de koopvaardij over de modderbanken in de Thames en aan Englelands oostkust. 'Thistle' is ook het enkel schip van deze typ, die in Schotland gebouwd werd - ze is naar het emblem van het land genoemd. Foto: Den Phillips

HENRYK RUTKOWSKI (Poland/*Polen*)

Normally she is used to give sailing opportunities to disabled people (like the' Lord Nelson'). She has friendly
rivalry with Ireland's 'Asgard` and the UK's 'Royalist' , in
these races, where she is a regular participant and
favourite.

*Im Einsatz für Segelreisen mit Behinderten (wie "Lord
Nelson") ist sie auch bei diesen Regatten regelmäßig als
Favorit dabei und kämpft mit der irischen "Asgard II" und
"Royalist" aus Großbritannien um die vordersten Plätze.*

Gewoonlijk nemmt ze gehandicapten naar zee (zoals de 'Lord
Nelson') en is in deze races een regelmatige deelnemer met veel
succes. 'Asgard II' (Ierland) en 'Royalist' (VK) zijn haar groote
maar vriendelijke concurrentie. Foto: Beken of Cowes.

MALCOLM MILLER

(Scotland/*Schottland*/Schotland)

Registered in Aberdeen, she was backed and named by the Lord Provost of Edinburgh and Lord Mayor of London in memory of his son. So many young men and women in the UK have cause to thank him for his generosity.

Dieses Schiff ist in Aberdeen registriert und wurde vom Lord Provost von Edinburgh und Lord Mayor von London zum Gedenken an seinen Sohn finanziert und benannt. Sehr viele junge Männer und Frauen sind diesem Mann zu Dank für seine Großzügigkeit verpflichtet.

Geregistreerd in Aberdeen, gesteund en gedoogpt de Lord Provost van Edinburgh en de Lord Mayor van Londen ter nagedachtenis aan zijn zoon. Foto: Beken of Cowes.

FRYDERYK CHOPIN (Poland/Polen)

Named after the famous composer, born and brought up
in Poland, she's fast - look at her long bowsprit, tall masts,
and many sails, which need careful handling..

*Benannt nach dem berühmten polnischen Komponisten. Ein
schnelles Schiff-mit einem langen Bugspriet, hohen Masten und
zahlreichen Segeln, die sorgfältig bedient werden müssen. .*

Genoemd naar de beroemde Poolse componist. Ze is
ontzettend snel-zie haar lange boegspriet, hoge masten en vele
zeilen war uiterst voorzichtig mee omgegaan moet worden.
Foto: Cutty Sark Scots Whisky.

ALEXANDER VON HUMBOLDT

(Germany/*Deutschland*/Duitsland)

For 80 years in the North Sea and Baltic as a lightship, she was converted between 1986 and 1988 by the German Sail Training Foundation with the help of sponsors. The splendid green of her hull was chosen as a traditional colour in Bremerhaven's shipbuilding. Now the youth of Germany enjoy her seakindliness.

Nach 80 Jahren Einsatz als Feuerschiff in der Nord- und Ostsee wurde sie zwischen 1986 und 1988 von der Deutschen Stiftung Sail Training und mit der Unterstützung von Sponsoren umgebaut. Das kräftige Grün ihres Rumpfes wurde als traditionelle Farbe des Bremerhavener Schiffbaus gewählt. Heute genießen deutsche Jugendliche die Seetüchtigkeit dieses Schiffs.

Ze heeft 80 jaren in de Noordzee en Baltische Zee als lichtschip doorgebracht en werd van 1986 to1988 omgebouwd door de Duitse Stichting Sail Training met de hulp van sponsors. Het schitterende groen van haar romp was gekózen als een traditio-neele kleur van de Bremerhavense scheepsbouw.. Nu kan de Duitse jeugd genieten van haar zeevriendelijkheid. Foto: Cutty Sark Scotch Whisky.

THOR HEYERDAHL

(Germany/*Deutschland*/Duitsland)

   Named after the famous explorer of the 'Kon Tiki', she engages in sail training and also chartering in the Carribean.

   Dieses Schiff ist nach dem berühmten „Kon-Tiki"-Forscher benannt benannt, fungiert als Segelschulschiff und nacht Winterfahrten in der Karibik.

   Genoemd naar de beroemde ontdekkingsreiziger van de 'KonTiki' en beschikbaar voor zeiltraining en eveneens voo chartertochten in de Carribische Oceaan.

SWAN FAN MAKKUM
(Netherlands/*Niederlande*/Nederland)

In the Baltic for the Summer and in the winter, she has
two week courses in the Carribean. Who can want more?
On day courses she takes up to 120 passengers, but for
long voyages, she takes 36. Built in Gdansk, Poland, she's
owned by V &S Charters.

*Im Sommer segelt sie in der Ostsee, im Winter führen zwei-
wöchige Törns durch die Karibik. Was kann schöner sein? Bei
Tagesfahiten sind bis zu 120 Passagiere an Bord, aber für län-
gere Reisen nur 36. Sie wurde in Gdansk/Polen gebaut, Eigner
ist V & S Charters.*

In de zomer maakt ze zeiltochten in de Baltische Zee, de winter brengt ze met twee weken lange tochten in de Carribische
Oceaan door-helemaal naar uw zin. Voor een dag neemt ze tot
120 pasagiers aan boord, op langere reizen alleen 36. Ze is
gebouwd in Gdansk/Polen en eigendom van V & S Charters.

SEDOV (Russia/*Rußland*/(Rusland)

Sedov's four masts tower above the others, and indeed she is the largest sailing ship in the world that still goes to sea. Now based in the Arctic's Murmansk, she appears at most sail training events. *Die vier Masten der „Sedov" überragen alle anderen Schiffe, und deshalb ist dies auch das größte immer noch seegängige Schiff. Sein Heimathafen ist Murmansk in der Arktik, und es nimmt an den meisten Segelschulveranstaltungen teil.*

De vier masten van de Sedov torenen boven alle anderen uit en ze is dan ook het grootste zeevarende zeilschip ter wereld. Ze heeft het Arctische Moermansk als thuishaven en komt uit voor bijna alle zeiltraininggebeurens. Foto: Cutty Sark Scots Whisky

POGORIA (Poland/*Polen*/Polen)

One of a number of sisterships, others include Kaliakra (Bulgaria) and Iskra (Poland). You'll recognise them from their distinctive wide sterns.

Dieses Schiff hat eine Reihe von Schwesterschiffen wie die „Kaliakra" (Bulgarien) und „Iskra" (Polen), die alle an ihrem deutlich breiten Spiegelheck erkennbar sind.

Een van een aantal gelijksoortige schepen, waaronder ook de Kaliakra (Bulgarije) en Iskra (Polen). Ze zijn te herkennen aan hun opvallend brede achtersteven. Foto: Beken of Cowes.

DAR MLODZIEZY (Poland/*Polen*/(Polen)

Poland's pride, her name meaning 'Gift of Youth'. Her longest voyage was to Australia for the Bicentennial Celebrations, returning in dramatic weather around Cape Horn.

Dieses Schiff, dessen Name „Geschenk der Jugend" bedeutet, ist Polens Stolz und hat Australien anläßlich seiner Zweihundertjahrfeier besucht und auf der Rückreise um Kap Hoorn schweres Wetter überstanden.

De trots van Polen met een naam die 'Cadeau van de Jeugd' betekent. Haar langste reis was naar Australië voor het tweehonderdjarig bestaan en tijdens de terugtocht rondde ze de Kaap Hoorn onder dramatische weersomstandigheden. Foto: Beken of Cowes.

Forth Estuary Forum

"1995 is a year of firsts"

For the first time ever, the Firth of Forth is hosting the Cutty Sark Tall Ships Race.

For the first time ever, the Firth of Forth is being cared for by a voluntary partnership.

Industries, organisations and individuals around the river are joining together to work for the future health and wealth of the Firth of Forth.

photo: P. & A. Macdonald

THE GROUP IS CALLED THE
FORTH ESTUARY FORUM -
A FIRST FOR THE PRESENT
AND LIKE THE TALL SHIPS,
CREATED TO LAST.

Get involved, contact:

Mark Jennison
   Secretary
   Forth Estuary Forum
Battleby
Perth PH1 3EW

Tel: 01738 444177
   Fax: 01738 444180

KRUZENSHTERN (Russia/*Rußland*/Rusland)

Built in 1926 as the 'Padua', one of the famous 'Flying P' windjammers, she used to carry nitrates from Chile, round Cape Horn. Her sistership ' Passat' is also afloat, at Travemunde. In the old days, to scare pirates, sides of ships were painted as if they were warships with guns.

Dieses 1926 unter dem Namen „Padua" gebaute und zur berühmten Windjammer-Baureihe „Flying P" gehörende Schiff wurde früher als Nitrat-Frachter von Chile um das Kap Hoorn herum eingesetzt. Ihr Schwesterschiff „Passat" mit liegt nodr in Travemünde. Früher wurden Schiffsseiten zur Abschreckung von Piraten so angestrichen, daß sie mit Kanonen bestückten Kriegsschiffen glichen.

Gebouwd in 1926 als de 'Padua', een van de beroemde 'Vliegende P' windjammers, en gebruikt om nitraten van Chili rond de Kaap Hoorn te vervoeren. Haar zusterschip de 'Passat' is ook nog steeds in het water, in Travemunde. In het verleden werden de zijkanten van schepen beschilderd alsof het oorlogschepen met kanonnen waren, om piraten af te schrikken.
Foto: Beken of Cowes

DANMARK (Denmark/*Dänemark*/Denemarken)

Denmark has two square riggers, the other is Georg Stage. They both train future merchant navy officers.

Dänemark besitzt zwei Schiffe mit Rahetakelung. Das zweite ist „Georg Stag". Beide Schiffe bilden Offiziere für die Handelsmarine aus.

Denemarken heeft twee vierkant getuigde schepen, de andere is de Georg Stage. Beide worden gebruikt voor het opleiden van toekomstige koopvaardij-officieren. Foto: Beken of Cowes

ROYALIST (UK/*Großbritannien*/VK)

She takes Sea Cadets to sea as an extension of their onshore and small boat training. Her rig provides excellent opportunities for her crew to exercise skill and daring.

Dieses Schiff bildet Seekadètten im Anschluß an ihre Ausbildung an Land und auf kleineren Booten weiter. Die Takelung bietet ausgezeichnete Gelegenheit für die Erprobung von Fachkenntissen und Mut.

Zij voert zeekadetten naar zee als vervolg op hun opleiding ter land en in kleine boten. Haar tuigage biedt de bemanning uitstekende kansen om hun vaardigheden en lef te vertonen. Foto:

Beken of Cowes.

JENS KROGH
(Denmark/*Dänemark*/Denemarken)

Built in 1899 in Frederikshavn as a fishing boat, Jens Krogh has been converted to a sail training ship for boys and girls from the surroundings of Aalborg.

Sie ist 1899 in Frederikshavn als Fischereifahrzeug gebaut und wurde für das Sail Training von Jungen und Mädchen aus der Umgebung von Aalborg umgestaltet.

Gebouwd in 1899 in Frederikshavn als een visserschip en gerestaureerd voor sail training van jongen en meisjes uit de buurt van Aalborg.

GLADAN (Sweden/*Schweden*/Zweden)

Gladan and her sistership FALKEN are both in this year's races. Gladan is a Swedish Royal Navy sail training ship, built at the Navy Dockyard, and has a two masted gaff schooner rig.

Sowohl die „Gladan" als auch ihr Schwesterschiff „Falken" nehmen an den diesjährigen Regatten teil. Die auf der Marinewerft gebaute „Gladan" ist ein Segelschulschiff der schwedischen Königlichen Marine und als Toppsegelschoner getakelt.

De Gladan en haar zusterschip de Falken verschijnen dit jaar alletwee aan de start. Gladan is een opleidingszeilschip van de Zweedse Koninklijke Marine dat op de Marinewerf gebouwd werd en heeft een Topzeil-Gaffelschoener tuigage. Foto: Beken of Cowes.

EENDRACHT (Netherlands/*Niederlande*/Nederland)

The second ship to carry this name, she is larger to give opportunities to even more young Dutch people..

Das zweite Schiff dieses Namens ist größer als das erste und bietet Ausbildungsmöglichkeiten für noch mehr Holländer.

Het tweede schip met deze naam. Ze is groter dan het eerste om nog meer Nederlandse jonge mensen een kans te geven.

Foto: Beken of Cowes,

KHERSONES (Ukraine/*Ukraine*/Oekraïne)

Her name originates from her home port on the Black Sea. Russian sisterships include Mir ('Peace'), Druzhba ('Friendship'), Pallada, Nadezhda ('Hope'), and the original ship, Dar Mlodziezy from Poland.

Die „Khersones" hat mehrere Schwesterschiffe wie die „Mir" (Frieden), die „Druschba" (Freundschaft), die „Pallada", die „Nadeschda" (Hoffnung) und das Originalschiff „Dar Mlodziezy" aus Polen.

Haar naam betekent eveneens haar thuishavn aar de Zwarte Zee. Russische zusterschepen zijn de Mir ('Vrede'), Druzhba ('Vriendschap'), Pallada, Nadezhda ('Hoof'), en het originele schip de Dar Mlodziezy uit Polen.

SIR WINSTON CHURCHILL

(UK/*Großbritannien*/VK)

Nearly 30 years old, she and her sistership Malcolm Miller have been the twins of the Sail Training Association fleet, taking thousands of youngsters to sea. A new ship for the STA starts building this year.

Dieses fast 30 Jahre alte Schiff und sein Schwesterschiff „Malcolm Miller" sind die Zwillinge der Flotte der „Sail Training Association" und haben Tausende Jugendliche mit der Hochsee bekannt gemacht. Ein weiteres Schiff der STA wird in diesem Jahr auf Kiel gelegt.

Ze is bijna dertig jaar oud en is samen met haar zusterschip de Malcolm Miller de tweeling van de Sail Training Association vloot, en heeft meer dan duizenden jongeren naar zee genomen. Met de bouw van een nieuw STA-schip wordt dit jaar begonnen.
Foto: Beken of Cowes

ASGARD II (Ireland/(Rep. Irland/Ierland)

Ireland established sail training in 1969, after lessons with the first Asgard and with Creidne. Asgard - 'Home of the Gods' in Norse - is a fine ambassador for her country.

Irland begründete das Sail Training im Jahre 1969 nach ersten Ausbildungsfahrten mit der ersten „Asgard" und der „Creidne". Die „Asgard" (Altnorwegisch für „Heimat der Götter") ist eine ausgezeichnete Botschafterin ihres Heimatlandes.

Ierland heeft zeiltraining in 1969 ingevoerd, na lessen met de eerste Asgard en met de Creidne. Asgard - 'Thuis van de Goden' in Norse - is een uitstekende ambassadeur voor haar land.

SPIRIT OF SCOTLAND

(Scotland/*Schottland*/ (Schotland)

Sponsored by Scottish Nuclear, she is a replica of an 1850 Liverpool Bay Pilot Schooner. She is owned by Fairbridge Trust, who work with youngsters (14-25) who are unwaged and deemed to be 'at risk'.

Dieses von „Scottish Nuclear" unterstützte Schiff ist eine Nachbildung des Lotsenschoners 'Liverpool Bay' der von 1850 und gehört dem „Fairbridge Trust", der arbeitslose und sozial gefährdete Jugendliche (14 bis 25 Jahre) fördert.

Gesponsord door Scottish Nuclear en een replica van een Loodsschoener uit de Baai van Liverpool uit 1850. Ze is het eigendom van het Fairbridge Trust dat jongeren (14-25) die werkeloos zijn en verder weinig kansen hebben, een uitdaging wil bieden.

DEN STORE BJØRN
(Denmark/*Dänemark*/Denemarken)

A long, thin three masted schooner, of 123 feet (37 metres) built in 1902, and she only sails with a crew of 2■

Ein 1902 gebauter langer, schlanker Dreimaster von 37 Metern (123 Fuß) Länge mit einer Besatzung von nur 20 Personen.

Een lange smalle schoener met drie masten en een lengte van 37 meter. Ze werd in 1902 gebouwd en heeft een bemanning van slechts 20. Foto Janka Bielak.

RETURN OF MARCO POLO
(UK/*Großbritannien*/VK)

Built as a lightship, she's been converted in almost the sam■ manner as 'Den Store Bjørn'. She is one of three ships owne■ by the Little School of Winestead, aiming to increase self esteem amongst pupils who had a disadvantaged start to life■

Das ehemalige Feuerschiff wurde ähnlich wie "Den Store Bjørn" umgebaut. Es ist eines von drei Schiffen der "Kleinen Schule von Winestead", deren Ziel es ist, das Selbstvertrauen der Schüler zu stärken, die bei ihrem Start ins Leben benachteiligt waren.

Gebouwd als lichtschip en omgebouwd zoals "Den Store Bjørn". ■ is een van drie schepen van de "Kleine school van Winestead". D■ bedoeling is het zelfvertrouwen van de jonge mensen te sterken, di■ een moeilijk start in het leven hadden.

OTRE DAME DES FLOTES
(France/*Frankreich*/Frankrijk)

urrah for having France's tricolor flag in this year's race,
sted by the crew of a fine white ketch.

*ir freuen uns sehr, in diesem Jahr auch wieder die französische
kolore zu sehen, die auf dieser schönen weißen Ketsch gefahren
d.*

n vriendelijk welkom aan de bemanning van deze fijne witte
el-kits, die haar tricolore vlag zal zetten. Foto: Beken of Cowes.

HAWILA (Sweden/*Schweden*/Zweden)

As with Astrid Finne she belongs to MBV (Towards better knowledge).

Auch dieses Schiff gehört MBV („Für besseres Wissen").
Evenals de Astrid Finne is zij het eigendom van MBV (Naar
betere kennis).

STRID FINNE (Sweden/*Schweden*/Zweden)

he belongs to the voluntary school sailing association.
V (Towards better knowledge).
*ieses Schiff gehört der Gemeinnützigen Segelschule MBV
Für besseres Wissen").*
e is het eigendom van de vrijwillige school-zeilvereniging
V (Naar betere kennis). Foto: L. Martinsson

ATLANTICA (Sweden/*Schweden*/Sweden)

Built 1981 on lines similar to GRATITUDE for SKS
Seglarskola, Gothenburg, Sweden, she is sailed by 24 trainees
and 8 permanent crew. A good and seaworthy hull with traditional sailing trawler rig. Sie wurde 1981 für die SKS
Segelschule in Göteborg/Schweden gebaut, in ihren Linien äh-
lich der GRATITUDE, und wird von 24 Trainees und einer
achtköpfigen Stammbesatzung gesegelt. Ihr starker,
ssetüchtiger Rumpf erhielt ein traditionelles Trawler-Rigg.
Ze werd 1981 voor de SKS Zeilschool in Gothenburg, Zwede
gebouwd en heeft 24 trainees en 8 vaste bemanning. En sterk
romp met een traditioneele treilerstuigage. Foto: M. Johansson

GRATITUDE (Sweden/*Schweden*/Sweden)

Built 1903 in Portleven does her 38th season as a sail training ship for SKS Seglarskola, Gothenburg, Sweden. Three times over-all winner, she will this year - as in the past -be crewed by girls.

Sie wurde 1903 in Portleven gebaut und hat 38 Jahre als Ausbildungsschiff für die SKS Segleschule in Göteborg/Schweden gedient. Dreimal war sie Gesamtsiegerin der Regatta, in diesem Jahr ist sie mit einer Mädchencrew dabei.

In 1903 gebouwd in Portleven en 38 jaren van dienst als een sail training schip voor de SKS zeilschool in Gotheburg, Zweden. Driemaal was ze over all-all winner en zal dit jaar een bemanning van meisjes hebben. Foto: L. Svensson

GROSSHERZOGIN ELISABETH
(Germany/*Deutschland*/Duitsland)

Built in 1908 she carries 62 people, and sails out of Elsfleth, not far from Bremen.

Dieses 1908 gebaute Schiff mit Heimathafen Elsfleth (a.d. Hunte bei Oldenburg) hat eine Besatzung von 62 Mann.

Dit schip werd in 1908 gebouwd, voert 62 mensen en heeft Elfleth, in de buurt van Bremen, als thuishaven. Foto: R. Wichmann.

EXCELSIOR (UK/*Großbritannien*/VK)

A fishing trawler from the East Coast of England (Lowestoft) she still is operated from there by the Excelsior Trust. *Dieser Hochsee-Trawler von der Ostküste Englands (Lowestoft) wird bis heute vom „Excelsior Trust" betrieben.*
Een visserstreiler van de oostkust van Engeland (Lowestoft) en werkt nog steeds vanuit deze haven onder de Excelsior Trust.
Foto: Andrew Thompson.

LORD NELSON (UK/*Großbritannien*/VK)

She's designed to take disabled people to sea , and she has lifts, and room along the deck for wheelchairs. Each disabled has an able bodied 'buddy', and they all play an active part in running the ship. *Dieses Schiff ist für eine aus körperbehinderten Personen zusammengesetzte Mannschaft ausgerüstet . Das Schiff hat Aufzüge und auf Deck Raum für Rollstühle. Jedes körperbehinderte Besatzungsmitglied hat einen „unversehrten" Partner, und alle Mitreisenden sind aktiv an der Führung des Schiffs beteiligt.* Ze is ontworpen om gehandicapten naar zee te nemen en ze heeft lifts, en ruimte op het dek voor rolstoelen. Iedere gehandicapte opvarende heeft een niet-gehandicapte 'buddy' en ze spelen allemaal een actieve rol in de running van het schip. Foto Beken of Cowes.

ROALD AMUNDSEN
(Germany/*Deutschland*/Duitsland)

She is today the only brig in Germany and was rebuilt by the association "Learn to Live on Sailing Ships". *Sie ist heute die einzige deutsche Brigg und wurde vom Verein "Leben Lernen auf Segelschiffen" umgebaut.* Ze is vandaag de enkele brik in Duitsland en werd omgebouwd door de vereniging "Leven Leren op Zeilschepen". Foto: Monika Kludas

SVYATITEL NIKOLAI
(Russia/*Rußland*/Rusland)

This three-masted ship from Petrosavodsk is named after Saint Nicholas. The "lodja" type was a characteristic sailing vessel on Russian rivers and lakes.

Dieser Dreimaster aus Petrosavodsk ist nach dem Heiligen Nikolaus benannt. Die "Lodja" war ein charakteristisches Segelschiff auf russischen Flüssen und Seen.

Dit driemast-schip uit Petrozavodsk is genoemd naar St. Niklaas. De "lodja" was een karakteristiek zeilschip op Russische rivieren en meren. Foto: Monika Klaudas.

SEUTE DEERN
(Germany/*Deutschland*/Duitsland)

Built in 1939 as a Baltic trader in Denmark. She has a crew of 30 and sails in the Baltic, North Sea and Atlantic. *Als Frachtsegler 1939 in Dänemark gebaut. Sie hat 30 Crewmitglieder und segelt in der Ost-und Nordsee sowie auf dem Atlantik.* 1939 als een vrachtzeilschip in Denemarken gebouwd. Ze heeft een bemanning van 30 en zeilt in de Baltische Zee, de Noordzee en de Atlantische Oceaan. Foto: Beken of Cowes.

SKIBLADNER
(Denmark/*Dänemark*/Denemarken)

One of the few ships built as long ago as the 1890's, she is a welcome entry.

Als eines der Traditionsschiffe, die um 1890 vom Stapel liefen, ist sie eine willkommene Teilnehmerin.

Als een van de schepen, die om 1890 van stapel liepen, is ze een welgezien deelnemer.

ZEELANDIA
(Netherlands/Niederlande/Nederland)
Foto Monika Kaludas.

JEAN DE LA LUNE
(Scotland/Scottland/Schotland)
Foto Steve Martin Collection.

NOBILE (Germany/*Deutschland*/Duitsland)

"Nobile" was launched in Lowestoft/Norfolk in 1919 as a fishing boat and was recently converted to a racing-cutter by the project "Learn To Live on Sailing Ships" in Wolgast/Germany. For the first time she participates in the Cutty Sark Tall Ships' Races. *"Nobile" lief 1919 in Lowestoft/Norfolk als Fischereisegler vom Stapel und wurde kürzlich vom Projekt "Leben Lemen auf Segelschiffen" zum Rennkutter umgebaut. Sie nimmt zum ersten Mal an den Cutty Sark Tall Ships' Races teil.* "Nobile" is gebouwd in Lowestoft/Norfolk in 1919 als een visserschip en wordt gerestaureerd als een race-kotter door het projekt "Leven Leren op Zeilschepen". Dit is haar eerste deelname aan de races. Foto: Monika Klaudas

Ships Participating...   Teilnehmende Schippe...   Deelnemende Schepen...

CLASS A: The largest ships which are either Square Rigged and over 120 feet (36.6 metres) in length, or are fore and aft rigged and over 160 feet (48.8 metres)
KLASSE A: Die großten Schiffe mit Rahetakelung und über 36,6 m Länge oder mit Schrat-Takelung und über 48,8 Länge.
KLASSE A: De Grootste schepen die getuigd zijn met ra-zeilen en een lengte van meer dan 36,6 meter hebben, of langsscheepsgetuigd metzijn zijn en een lengte van meer dan 48,8 meter hebben.

Name of ship Schiffsname Schiffsname (Nation/Land/Vlag)	Length of hull (metres) Rumpflänge Romplengte	Length of bowsprit (metres) Bugsprietlänge Boegsprietlengte	Number of masts Anzahl maste Aantal masten	Rig Takelung Tuigage	Hull colour Rumpffarbe Kleur van de romp	Sail number Segelnummer Zeilnummer	Construction date Baujahr Bouwjaar	Owner Eigner Eigenaar	Ports to be visited Anzulaufende Häfen Te bezoekende Havens
ALEXANDER VON HUMBOLDT (Germany/Deutschland/Duitsland)	54.2	8.5	2	Barque/Bark	Green Grün Groen	TSG 404	1906	Sail Training Association (Germany)	EBFAZ
CHRISTIAN RADICH (Norway/Norwegen/Noorwegen)	63.9	8.2	3	Ship/Vollshiff/ Volschip	White Weiß Wit		1937	S/S C.Radich	BA
DANMARK (Denmark/Dänemark/Denemarken)	76	9.5	3	Ship/Vollshiff/ Volschip	White Weiß Wit		1933	Danish Maritime Authority	FA
DAR MLODZIEZY (Poland/Polen)	94.4	15.2	3	Ship/Vollshiff/ Volschip	White Weiß Wit		1982	Merchant Marine Academy	EBFAZ
EENDRACHT (Netherlands/Niederlande/Nederland)	55.4	3.6	3	Schooner/Schoner Schoener	Blue Blau Blauw	TSH 477	1989	Stichting Het Zeilend Zeeschip	EBFA
FRYDERYK CHOPIN (Poland/Polen)	43.8	10.6	2	Brig/Brigg/Brik	White/Red Weiß/ Rot Wit/Rood	PZ 2777	1990	International Class Float	EBFAZ
GROSSHERZOGIN ELISABETH (Germany/Deutschland/Duitsland)	52.9	11.5	3	Schooner/Schoner Schoener	White Weiß Wit	TS 199	1908	Schulschiffverein	EB
KHERSONES (Ukraine/Oekraïne)	94.4	15.2	3	Ship/Vollschiff/ Volschip	White Weiß Wit		1989	Kerch Marine Technological Institute	BFA
KRUZENSHTERN (Russia/Rußland/Rusland)	104.1	9.1	4	Barque/Bark Bark	Blk/White Schwarz/ Weiß Zwart/Wit		1926	Baltic State Fishing Fleet	EBF
LORD NELSON (UK/Großbritannien/VK)	42.6	5.1	3	Barque/Bark Bark	Black Schwarz Zwart		1985	Jubilee Sailing Trust	EBFAZ
POGORIA (Poland/Polen)	41.1	8.5	3	Barquentine/Bark- schoner/Barkentijn	White Weiß Wit	PZ 1980	1980	Polish Yachting Association	EBFAZ
ROALD AMUNDSEN (Germany/Deutschland/Duitsland)	42	8	2	Brig/Brigg/Brik	Black Schwarz Zwart	TSG508	1952	Segelschiff Fridtjof Nansen	EB
SAGRES (Portugal)	81.6	7.3	3	Barque/Bark Bark	White Weiß Wit		1937	Portuguese Navy	EBFAZ
SEDOV (Russia/Rußland/Rusland)	108.7	13.7	4	Barque/Bark Bark	White Weiß Wit		1921	State Marine Academy	EBFAZ
SWAN FAN MAKKUM (Netherlands/Niederlande/Nederland)	49.6	10.3	2	Brigantine/ Brigantijn	Black Schwarz Zwart	TSH 511	1993	Swan Company - Holland	EBFAZ

Not all ships go to every port. See right hand column
Nicht alle Schippe laufen jeden Hafen an. Vlg. rechte Spalte
Niet alle schepen doen alle havens aan. Zie rechter kolom

E=Edinburgh   B=Bremerhaven   F=Frederikshavn   A=Amsterdam   Z=Zeebrugge

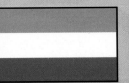
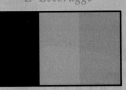

CLASS AII: This class is for Square Rigged ships, under 120 feet (36.6 metres).
KLASSE AII: Zu dieser klasse gehören alle Rahetakeling Schiffe unter 36,6m Länge
KLASSE AII: Deze klasse is voor schepen getuigd met ra-zeilen en van minder den 36,6 meter in lengte

Name of ship Schiffsname Schiffsname (Nation/Land/Vlag)	Length of hull (metres) Rumpflänge Romplengte	Length of bowsprit (metres) Bugsprietlänge Boegsprietlengte	Number of masts Anzahl maste Aantal masten	Rig Takelung Tuigage	Hull colour Rumpffarbe Kleur van de romp	Sail number Segelnummer Zeilnummer	Construction date Baujahr Bouwjaar	Owner Eigner Eigenaar	Ports to be visited Anzulaufende Häfen Te bezoekende Havens
ASGARD II (Ireland/Republik Irland/Ierland)	26.8	4.5	2	Brigantine/ Brigantijn	Green/Grün/ Groen	TSIR 15	1981	Coiste an Asgard	EBFAZ
HENRYK RUTKOWSKI (Poland/Polen)	24.0	4.5	2	Brigantine/ Brigantijn	Blk/White Schwarz/ Weiß Zwart/Wit	PZ 5	1944	Polish Yachting Association	EBFA
JEAN DE LA LUNE (UK/Großbritannien/VK)	23.8	6.1	2	Brigantine/ Brigantijn	Blue Blau Blauw		1957	Capt John Reid	EBFA
ROYALIST (UK/Großbritannien/VK)	23.4	4.8	2	Brig/Brigg/Brik	Blk/White Schwarz/ Weiß Zwart/Wit	TSK 23	1971	Sea Cadet Association	EBF
SVYATITEL NIKOLAI (Russia/Rußland/Rusland)	24.0	4.5	3	Caravel(lateen)Lat- einerigg/Latijn tuigage	Black Schwarz Zwart		1992	'Karelai-Tamp'	BFAZ
TRADEWIND (Finland/Finnland)				Schooner/Schoner Schoener	Black Schwarz Zwart		1911	Cristian Johannson	EBFA

CLASS B: All Fore and Aft rigged ships between 100 and 160 feet (30.5 metres and 48.8 metres) in length
KLASSE B: Alle schiffe mit Schrat-Takeling zwischen 30,5 bis 48,8 m Länge
KLASSE B: Alle schepen met Langsscheepse Tuigage en tussen 30,5 en 48,8 meter lengte

Name of ship Schiffsname Schiffsname (Nation/Land/Vlag)	Length of hull (metres) Rumpflänge Romplengte	Length of bowsprit (metres) Bugsprietlänge Boegsprietlengte	Number of masts Anzahl maste Aantal masten	Rig Takelung Tuigage	Hull colour Rumpffarbe Kleur van de romp	Sail number Segelnummer Zeilnummer	Construction date Baujahr Bouwjaar	Owner Eigner Eigenaar	Ports to be visited Anzulaufende Häfen Te bezoekende Havens
DEN STORE BJØRN (Denmark/Dänemark/Denmarken)	37.4	11.8	3	Schooner/Schoner Schoener	Black Schwarz Zwart	TSD 516	1902	Småskolen Søfolkene	EBFA
FALKEN (Sweden/Schweden/Zweden)	34.4	5.4	2	Schooner/Schoner Schoener	White Weiß Wit	SO 2	1947	Royal Swedish Navy	EB
GLADAN (Sweden/Schweden/Zweden)	34.4	5.4	2	Schooner/Schoner Schoener	White Weiß Wit	SO 1	1947	Royal Swedish Navy	EB
JOHANN SMIDT (Germany/Deutschland/Duitsland)	32.8	3.0	2	Schooner/Schoner Schoener	Blue/White Blau/ Weib Blauw/Wit	TSG 47	1974	Clipper DJS	EBFA
MALCOLM MILLER (UK/Großbritannien/VK)	41.1	4.2	3	Schooner/Schoner Schoener	Black Schwarz Zwart	TSK 2	1968	Sail Training Association	EBFA
OOSTERSCHELDE (Netherlands/Niederlande/Nederland)	40.5	8	3	Schooner/Schoner Schoener	Blk/White Schwarz/ Weiß Zwart/Wit		1918	BV Reederij	EBFAZ
RETURN OF MARCO POLO (UK/Großbritannien/VK)	37.4	11.8	3	Schooner/Schoner Schoener	Black Schwarz Zwart	TSK 535	1907	The Small School at Winestead	EBFA
SIR WINSTON CHURCHILL (UK/Großbritannien/VK)	41.1	4.2	3	Schooner/Schoner Schoener	Black Schwarz Zwart	TSK 1	1966	Sail Training Association	EBFA
THOR HEYERDAHL (Germany/Deutschland/Duitsland)	42.6	7.3	3	Schooner/Schoner Schoener	Black Schwarz Zwart	TSG 342	1930	Segelschiff Thor Heyerdahl e.V	EBFA
YUNYI BALTIETS (Russia/Rußland/Rusland)	42.6	6.4	2	Schooner/Schoner Schoener	Black Schwarz Zwart		1989	Seea Club Yunga	EB
ZEELANDIA (Netherlands/Niederlande/Nederland)	32.8	6.1	2	Schooner/Schoner Schoener	Black Schwarz Zwart	TSH 499	1931	Marnix van der Wel	EBFAZ

see the World

On Ocean Youth Club's Round the World Voyage

1996

Canaries – January
Caribbean – February
Panama – March
Tahiti – May
Auckland – June
Australia – July
Mauritius – November
Cape Town – December

1997

Dakar – January
Azores – February

For more details about the World Voyage, visit OYC's stand at Leith, north side of Albert Dock, 15-18 July. OYC yachts **TAIKOO** and **SPIRIT OF BOADICEA** are in the dock area.

or call 01705 528421

Ocean Youth Club – an Educational Charity No. 306078

CLASS C: Division I. All gaff rigged ships of less than 100 feet (30.5 metres) length of hull not racing with spinnakers and all vessels built before 1939 not already included in Classes A, AII and B.
KLASSE C: Abteilung I. Alle gaffeltakelten Fahrzeuge von weniger als 30,5m Länge die keine Spinnaker benutzen, und alle Segelfahrzeuge, die vor 1939 gebaut wurden und noch nicht in den Klassen A, AII und B eingeschlossen sind.
KLASSE C: Divisie I. Alle met gaffelzeilen getuigden schepen van minder dan 30,5m lengte, die zonder spinnakers zeilen, en alle zeilvaartuigen, die voor 1939 gebouwd werden en noch niet in de klassen A, AII of B inbegrepen zijn.

Name of ship Schiffsname Schiffsname (Nation/Land/Vlag)	Length of hull (metres) Rumpflänge Romplengte	Length of bowsprit (metres) Bugsprietlänge Boegsprietlengte	Number of masts Anzahl maste Aantal masten	Rig Takelung Tuigage	Hull colour Rumpffarbe Kleur van de romp	Sail number Segelnummer Zeilnummer	Construction date Baujahr Bouwjaar	Owner Eigner Eigenaar	Ports to be visited Anzulaufende Häfen Te bezoekende Havens
ANYWAY (Netherlands/Niederlande/Nederland)	15.2	2.8	2	Schooner/Schoner Schoener	Black Schwarz Zwart		1983	Mr W.Brudon	EBFAZ
ASTRID FINNE (Sweden/Schweden/Zweden)	18.8	4.1	2	Ketch/Ketsch Kits	White Weiß Wit	RS 43	1937	MOT Battre Vetande	EBFAZ
ATLANTICA (Sweden/Schweden/Zweden)	26.4	7.6	2	Ketch/Ketsch Kits	Blue Blau Blauw	22	1981	SKS	EB
BALTIC BEAUTY (Sweden/Schweden/Zweden)	29.2	7.9	2	Ketch/Ketsch Kits	Blue Blau Blauw	6	1926	Yngve Victor Gottlow	BFAZ
CAROLA TRAVEMUNDE (Germany/Deutschland/Duitsland)	17.3	5.2	2	Ketch/Ketsch Kits	Black Schwarz Zwart	TSG 73	1900	Reith & Co	EBF
EXCELSIOR (UK/Großbritannien/VK)	23.4	6.1	2	Ketch/Ketsch Kits	Black Schwarz Zwart	LT 472	1921	The Excelsior Trust	EBFA
GOLDEN VANITY (UK/Großbritannien/VK)	11.8	3.0	1	Cutter/Kutter Kotter	Grey Grau Grijs	B M	1908	Golden Vanity Trust	EBFAZ
GRATITUDE (Sweden/Schweden/Zweden)	23.1	6.1	2	Ketch/Ketsch Kits	Blue Blau Blauw	4	1900	SKS	EB
HAWILA (Sweden/Schweden/Zweden)	25.8	7.9	2	Ketch/Ketsch Kits	Black Schwarz Zwart	TSS 374	1935	Mot Battre Vetande	EBF
JENS KROGH (Denmark/Dänemark/Denemarken)	18.5	5.4	2	Ketch/Ketsch Kits	White Weiß Wit	TSD 145	1899	FDF/FPF Aalborg sokreds	EBF
KLAUS STORTEBEKER III (Germany/Deutschland/Duitsland)	12.4	2.7	2	Ketch/Ketsch Kits	White Weiß Wit	TSG 379	1921	Klaus Vogel	EBFA
MORNING STAR OF REVELATION (UK/Großbritannien/VK)	16.4	2.7	2	Ketch/Ketsch Kits	White Weiß Wit	TSK 182	1978	Morning Star Trust	EBFA
MOWE (Germany/Deutschland/Duitsland)	12.2	2.7	2	Ketch/Ketsch Kits	Blk/Red Schwarz/ Rot Zwart/Rood	TSG 378	1943	Uta Eickhorst	EBF
NOBILE (Germany/Deutschland/Duitsland)	29.8	9.7	1	Cutter/Kutter Kotter	White Weiß Wit	TSG 514	1919	Leben Lernen Segelschiffen e.V	EBFAZ
NOTRE DAME DES FLOTS (France/Frankreich/Frankrijk)	20.7	5.2	2	Ketch/Ketsch Kits	White Weiß Wit	TSF 518	1951	Jean Paul Despres	EBFA
PANDORA (Netherlands/Niederlande/Nederland)	15.8	4	2	Ketch/Ketsch Kits	Blue Blau Blauw	TSH 421	1980	B B Veenstra	FAZ
REGINA GERMANIA (Germany/Deutschland/Duitsland)	13.7	1.8	2	Schooner/Schoner Schoener	Orange Oranje	TSG 432	1984	Eric Herrmann	EBFAZ
SANDEFJORD (Norway/Norwegen/Noorwegen)	14.6	4.3	2	Ketch/Ketsch Kits	White Weiß Wit	RS 28	1913	Gunn von Trepka	EBF
SEUTE DEERN (Germany/Deutschland/Duitsland)	30.1	6.1	2	Ketch/Ketsch Kits	Black Schwarz Zwart	TSG 43	1939	Clipper D J S	EBF
SKIBLADNER II (Denmark/Dänemark/Denemarken)	18.6	7.6	2	Ketch/Ketsch Kits	Black Schwarz Zwart	TSD 500	1897	FDF/FPF Kobenhavns Sokreds	EBFA
SPIRIT OF SCOTLAND (UK/Großbritannien/VK)	21.9	6.1	2	Schooner/Schoner Schoener	Blue Blau Blauw	TSK 381	1985	Fairbridge	EB
SWANTJE (Germany/Deutschland/Duitsland)	14.6	3.0	2	Ketch/Ketsch Kits	White Weiß Wit	TSG 336	1977	Segelschule Kapitan Kruse & Co	EBF
THISTLE (UK/Großbritannien/VK)	28		2	Barge/Platt- bodenschiff	Black Schwarz Zwart		1895	Thames Steam & Navigation	EB

Now Holland, without clogs.

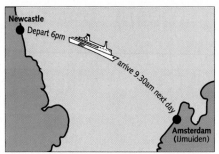

Newcastle
Depart 6pm
arrive 9.30am next day
Amsterdam
(IJmuiden)

Scandinavian Seaways now have a regular crossing from Newcastle to Amsterdam (IJmuiden) – so you can go Dutch without getting clogged up in the traffic on the long drive to the South Coast. Instead you can relax aboard a sleek white Scandinavian Seaways TravelLiner and cruise away to the land of the tulips in air conditioned comfort, enjoying Scandinavian hospitality all the way.

How about some smörgåsbord? There's always plenty going on with our on-board entertainment for young and old alike. Then enjoy a restful night's sleep in your cabin arriving fresh and ready for the open road at 09.30 next morning. It's the perfect way to get straight to the heart of Amsterdam for a break or as the start to a motoring holiday in Holland, Germany or beyond.

Return price for 4 people in a car from
£329
4 night City breaks per person from £139.
8 night family holidays per person from £137.
Departures every other day. See brochure for full schedule details.

☎ **01255 240 240**
Monday - Friday 8.30 - 20.00; Saturday 8.30 - 17.00; Sunday 10.00 - 16.00.

For further details call our 24-hour brochure line on 0117 944 7733 (quote ref 95/PN1208). Book through your travel agent or call 01255 240 240.

SCANDINAVIAN
SEAWAYS
A BETTER WAY OF TRAVELLING

CLASS C: Division II All ships with Bermudian rig under 100 feet (30.5 metres) in length, not using spinnakers.
KLASSE C: Abteilung II Alle shiffe mit Focktakelung unter 30,5 m Lange ohne spinnaker.
KLASSE C: Divisie II Alle schepen met grotzeilen en niet langer dan 30,5m, die zonder spinnaker zeilen.

Name of ship Schiffsname Schiffsname (Nation/Land/Vlag)	Length of hull (metres) Rumpflänge Romplengte	Length of bowsprit (metres) Bugsprietlänge Boegsprietlengte	Number of masts Anzahl maste Aantal masten	Rig Takelung Tuigage	Hull colour Rumpffarbe Kleur van de romp	Sail number Segelnummer Zeilnummer	Construction date Baujahr Bouwjaar	Owner Eigner Eigenaar	Ports to be visited Anzulaufende Häfen Te bezoekende Havens
ADAM (Belize)	8.8		2	Ketch/Ketsch Kits	White Weiß Wit	TS 8021	1994	Trans Line Shipping Company	EBFAZ
ARETHUSA (UK/Großbritannien/VK)	21.9		2	Ketch/Ketsch Kits	Blue Blau Blauw	TSK 198	1982	Shaftesbury Homes and Arethusa	EBFA
ATALANTE (UK/Großbritannien/VK)	28		2	Ketch/Ketsch Kits	White Weiß Wit	172	1961	Cabot Shipping Co	EBFAZ
BALDER Netherlands/Niederlande/Nederland)	17	4	2	Schooner/Schoner Schoener	Blue Blau Blauw	TSH 521	1983	J J Tiets	FAZ
DARK HORSE (UK/Großbritannien/VK)	17		2	Schooner/Schoner Schoener	White Weiß Wit	GBR 124	1979	Lloyds Bank Plc	EBFA
DIANA (Germany/Deutschland/Duitsland)	17.6		1	Sloop/Slup Sloep	Brown Braum Bruin	TSG 337	1980	H Bultjer	EB
ELENA-MARIA-BARBARA (Russia/Rußland/Rusland)	18.3	9.7	2	Schooner/Schoner Schoener	Blk/yellow Schwarz gelb Zwart/geel		1995	Alevtima Smetanina	EBFAZ
FIRST EXPERIENCE (UK/Großbritannien/VK)	15.8		1	Sloop/Slup Sloep	White Weiß Wit	5100 C	1989	Bob Moncur	EB
HARTLEPOOL RENAISSANCE (UK/Großbritannien/VK)	21.9		2	Ketch/Ketsch Kits	Red Rot Rood	TSK 438	1976	The Faramir Trust	EB
MAPLIN BIRD (UK/Großbritannien/VK)	13.7		2	Ketch/Ketsch Kits	Green Grün Groen	TSK 422	1982	Ian Griffiths	FAZ
MOKOTOW (Poland/Polen)	14		2	Yawl	Brown Braum Bruin	PZ 849	1977	Yacht Club of Poland, Warsaw	EBFAZ
NOMAD (Netherlands/Niederlande/Nederland)	15.2		1	Cutter/Kutter Kotter	Dark blu/Dunken-blau/Donkernblouw	048	1990	E M Markus	EBFAZ
OCEAN SCOUT (UK/Großbritannien/VK)	14.9		2	Ketch/Ketsch Kits	Blue Blau Blauw	TSK 494	1993	Scouts Offshore	EBFAZ
OCEAN VENTURE (UK/Großbritannien/VK)	17		2	Schooner/Schoner Schoener	White Weiß Wit	5237Y	1979	Malvern College	EBFA
ORION (Netherlands/Niederlande/Nederland)	11.9		1	Cutter/Kutter Kotter	White Weiß Wit	TSH 357	1991	J J Westerbeek	EBFAZ
OTAMA II (Australia/Australien/Australië)	15.2		1	Cutter/Kutter Kotter	White Weiß Wit	TSKA 48	1987	Farnham College/ Guildford School	EBFAZ
PETER VON DANZIG (Germany/Deutschland/Duitsland)	11		1	Sloop/Slup Sloep	Blue Blau Blauw	G 2200	1975	T & P Schmid	EBFA
RONA II (UK/Großbritannien/VK)	20.5		2	Ketch/Ketsch Kits	White Weiß Wit	TSK 435	1991	London Sailing Project	EBFA
SALEX (UK/Großbritannien/VK)	14		1	Cutter/Kutter Kotter	Blue Blau Blauw	K 300	1971	Scouts Offshore	EBFAZ
SMIAKY (Poland/Polen)	18		2	Ketch/Ketsch Kits	White Weiß Wit	PZ 25	1960	Sail Training Centre Poland	EBFA
SPIRIT OF BOADICEA (UK/Großbritannien/VK)	21.9		2	Ketch/Ketsch Kits	Blue Blau Blauw	OYC 7	1974	Ocean Youth Club	EBFAZ
TAIKOO (UK/Großbritannien/VK)	21.9		2	Ketch/Ketsch Kits	White Weiß Wit	OYC 5	1973	Ocean Youth Club	EBFAZ
ZVEZDA (Russia/Rußland/Rusland)	17		2	Ketch/Ketsch Kits	White Weiß Wit		1934	St Petersburg Yacht Club	EBFAZ
Also/auch BOA ESPERANÇA (Portugal)	26.5		2	Caravel(lateen)Lat-einrigg/Latijn tuigage	Black Schwarz Zwart		1990	Aporvela	BAZ

CLASS C: Division III All ships (with Bermudian rig) under 100 feet (30.5 metres) in length, racing with spinnakers.
KLASSE C: Abteilung III Alle (hochgetakelten) schiffe unter 30,5m mit spinnaker Länge, due mit spinnakem segeln.
KLASSE C: Divisie III alle schepen (met Bermuda Tuigage en) van minder dan 30,5 meter lemgte die met spinnakers zei den.

Name of ship Schiffsname Schiffsname (Nation/Land/Vlag)	Length of hull (metres) Rumpflänge Romplengte	Length of bowsprit (metres) Bugsprietlänge Boegsprietlengte	Number of masts Anzahl maste Aantal masten	Rig Takelung Tuigage	Hull colour Rumpffarbe Kleur van de romp	Sail number Segelnummer Zeilnummer	Construction date Baujahr Bouwjaar	Owner Eigner Eigenaar	Ports to be visited Anzulaufende Häfen Te bezoekende Havens
ADVENTURE (UK/Großbritannien/VK)	16.7	5	1	Cutter/Kutter Kotter	Blue Blau Blauw	GBR 3138	1971	J.S.A.S.T.C.	EBFA
AKELA (Russia/Rußland/Rusland)	13.7		1	Sloop/Slup Sloep	White Weiß Wit	SR 991	1986	Univercite of Water Comms	EBFAZ
BLACK DIAMOND OF DURHAM (UK/Großbritannien/VK)	13.7		1	Sloop/Slup Sloep	Black Schwartz Zwart	K3166	1973	The Faramir Trust	EBFAZ
BRITISH STEEL (UK/Großbritannien/VK)	18		2	Ketch/Ketsch Kits	Blue Blau Blauw	K 3388	1970	Royal Artillery Yacht Club	EBFAZ
BYLINA (Russia/Rußland/Rusland)	12.5		1	Sloop/Slup Sloep	White Weiß Wit	SR 750	1975	Admiral Makarov Maritime Academy	EBFAZ
DASHER (UK/Großbritannien/VK)	16.4		1	Cutter/Kutter Kotter	Blue Blau Blauw	K 1204	1977	J S A S T C	EBFA
GALAHAD (UK/Großbritannien/VK)	11.9		1	Sloop/Slup Sloep	White Weiß Wit	K 2531	1983	RN Engineering College	EBFAZ
GRENADA (Estonia/Estland/Estonië)	12.2		1	Sloop/Slup Sloep	White Weiß Wit	EST 81	1965	Baltsail Club	EBFAZ
HAJDUK (Poland/Polen)	13.1		1	Sloop/Slup Sloep	Blue Blau Blauw	PZ 808	1977	Morski Klub Sportowy Pogon	EBFAZ
HELENA CRISTINA (Netherlands/Niederlande/Nederland)	14.3		2	Ketch/Ketsch Kits	White Weiß Wit	TSH 535	1986	Arie Trust	EBFAZ
LORD TRENCHARD (UK/Großbritannien/VK)	16.7		2	Yawl	White Weiß Wit	K 3197	1973	Royal Air Force	EBFA
MARABU (UK/Großbritannien/VK)	17.7		2	Ketch/Ketsch Kits	Blue Blau Blauw	5625 Y	1935	Marabu Syndicate	EBF
RUS (Russia/Rußland/Rusland)	10.7		1	Sloop/Slup Sloep	White Weiß Wit	SR909	1973	Baltic Shipping Company	FA
S:T IV (Sweden./Schweden/Zweden)	12.2		1	Sloop/Slup Sloep	White Weiß Wit	S 17	1990	Antenn 14 Sailing AB	EBFA
SARIE MARAIS OF PLYMOUTH (UK/Großbritannien/VK)	11.9		1	Sloop/Slup Sloep	White Weiß Wit		1993	Mr R Kay	EBFAZ
SPARTA (Latvia/Lettland)	16.7		1	Sloop/Slup Sloep	White Weiß Wit	SR 936	1977	Latvian Shipping Co.	EBFA
SOPHIA (Russia/Rußland/Rusland)	11.6		1	Sloop/Slup Sloep	White Weiß Wit	RUS 635	1993	Admiral Makarov Maritime Academy	EBFAZ
STELLA POLARE (Italy/Italien/Italië)	21.6		2	Yawl	White Weiß Wit	I 4519	1965	Italian Naval Academy	EBFAZ
SVANEN (Denmark/Dänemark//Denemarken)	19.5		1	Yawl	White Weiß Wit	D 101	1961	Danish Training Squadron	FA
THYRA (Denmark/Dänemark/Denemarken)	19.5		1	Yawl	White Weiß Wit	D 102	1961	Danish Training Squadron	FA
TORNADO (Poland/Polen)	17.7		1	Sloop/Slup Sloep	White Weiß Wit	PZ 41	1972	J KM Kotwica Gdynia	FA
URANIA (Netherlands/Niederlande/Nederland)	22	1.8	2	Ketch/Ketsch Kits	White Weiß Wit	H 31	1928	Royal Netherlands Navy	EBFAZ
VEGEWIND (Germany/Deutschland/Duitsland)	19.8	0.9	2	Schooner/Schoner Schoener	Blue Blau Blauw	TSG 509	1992	Aucoop Bootswerkstaat Bremen	EBFAZ
WALROSS III BERLIN (Germany/Deutschland/Duitsland)	16.1		1	Sloop/Slup Sloep	White Weiß Wit	G 909	1971	Claus Reichardt	EB
WANDELAAR III (Belgium/Belgien/België)	13.7		1	Sloop/Slup Sloep	Red Rot Rood	490	1979	Looman N V	EBFAZ

Rigs / *Takelung* / Tuigage

Square rig
Rahtakelung
Ra-zeilen

Fore and aft rig
Schrat-Takelung
Langsscheepse Tuigage

Length of bowsprit
Bugsprietlänge
Boegsprietlengte

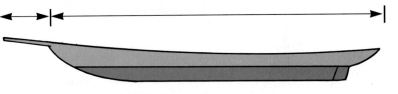

Length of hull
Rumpflänge
Romplengte

Sails / *Segel* / Zeilen

Spinnaker
Spinnaker
Spinnaker

Mainsail
Großsegel
Grootzeil

Foresail
Vorsegel
Voorzeil

Bermudian rig
Hochtakelung
Toren (Bermuda) tuigage

Gaff rig
Gaffeltakelung
Gaffelzeilen

Rigs / *Takelung* / Tuigage

"FREEDOM RIG"
„*FREEDOMRIG*"
"FREEDOM"

CUTTER
KUTTER
KOTTER

LATEEN RIG
LATEINERRIGG
LATIJN TUIGAGE

One mast, two or more foresails
Ein Mast, zwei oder mehr Vorsegel
Een mast, twee of meer voorzeilen

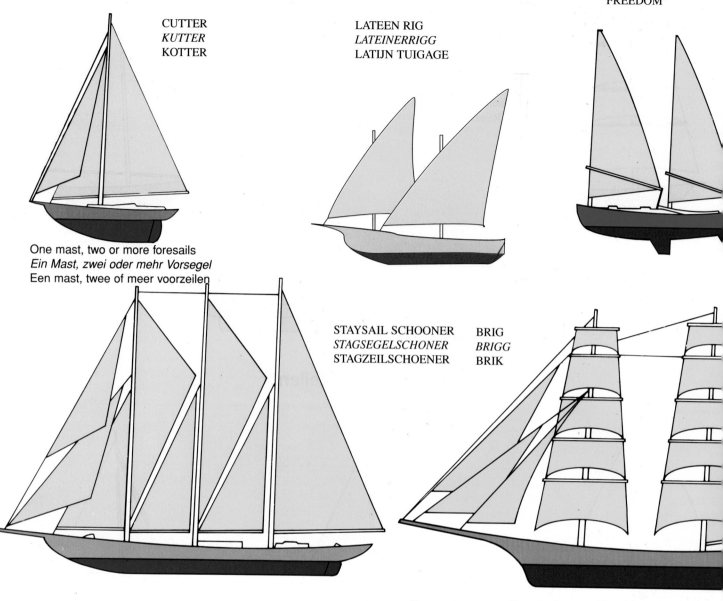

STAYSAIL SCHOONER
STAGSEGELSCHONER
STAGZEILSCHOENER

BRIG
BRIGG
BRIK

Two masts, square sails on both masts *Zwei Masten, Rahsegel an beiden Masten* Twee masten, razeilen aan beide masten

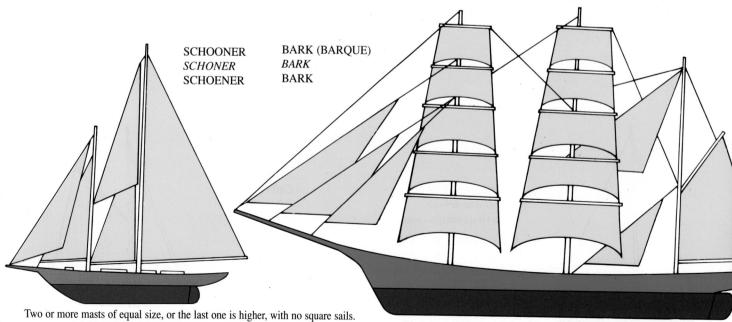

SCHOONER
SCHONER
SCHOENER

BARK (BARQUE)
BARK
BARK

Two or more masts of equal size, or the last one is higher, with no square sails. *Zwei oder mehr Masten gleicher Höhe, oder der achtere Mast ist höher, keine Rahsegel* Twee of meer masten van gelijke grootte, of waarvan de tweede mast groter is, zonder razeilen.

Three or more masts, with square sails, but not on the last mast. *Drei oder mehr Masten mit Rahsegeln, aber nicht am achteren Mast* Drie of meer masten, met razeilen, maar niet aan de laatste mast.

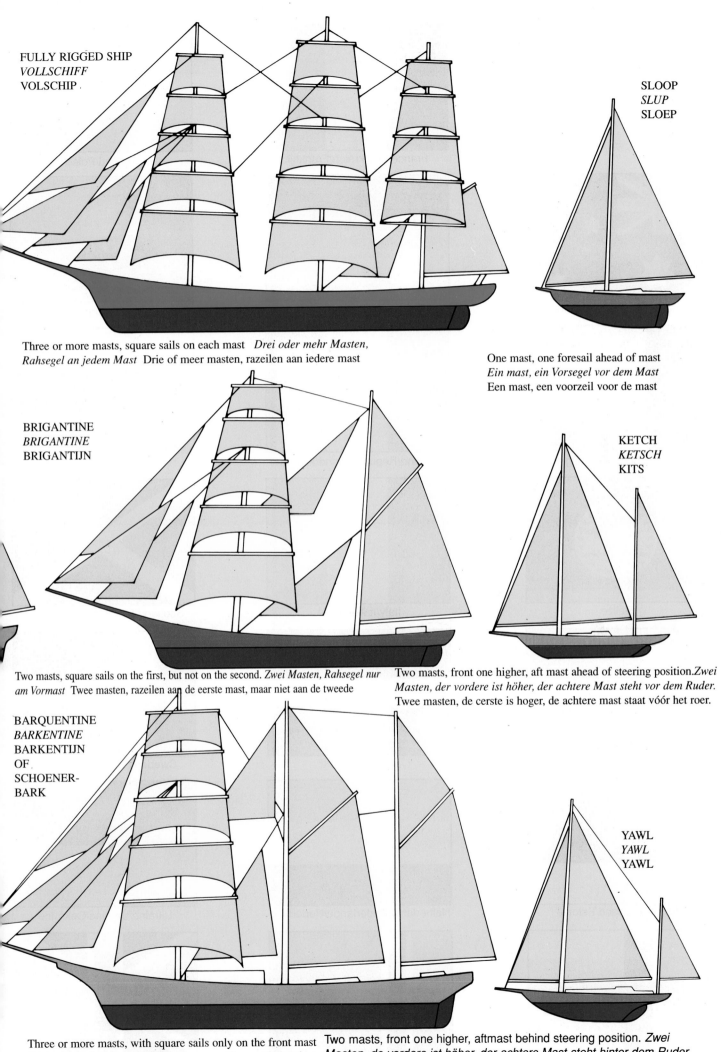

FULLY RIGGED SHIP
VOLLSCHIFF
VOLSCHIP

SLOOP
SLUP
SLOEP

Three or more masts, square sails on each mast *Drei oder mehr Masten, Rahsegel an jedem Mast* Drie of meer masten, razeilen aan iedere mast

One mast, one foresail ahead of mast
Ein mast, ein Vorsegel vor dem Mast
Een mast, een voorzeil voor de mast

BRIGANTINE
BRIGANTINE
BRIGANTIJN

KETCH
KETSCH
KITS

Two masts, square sails on the first, but not on the second. *Zwei Masten, Rahsegel nur am Vormast* Twee masten, razeilen aan de eerste mast, maar niet aan de tweede

Two masts, front one higher, aft mast ahead of steering position.*Zwei Masten, der vordere ist höher, der achtere Mast steht vor dem Ruder.* Twee masten, de cerste is hoger, de achtere mast staat vóór het roer.

BARQUENTINE
BARKENTINE
BARKENTIJN
OF
SCHOENER-
BARK

YAWL
YAWL
YAWL

Three or more masts, with square sails only on the front mast *Drei oder mehr Masten, Rahsegel nur am Vormast* Drie of meer masten, met razeilen alleen aan de eerste mast

Two masts, front one higher, aftmast behind steering position. *Zwei Masten, de vordere ist höher, der achtere Mast steht hinter dem Ruder.* Twee masten, de cerste is hoger, de achtere staat achter het roer

- *Recognise Ships from their National Flags*
- *An diesen Flaggen Können Sie die Herkunft der Schiffe erkennen*
- *Herken Schepen aan hun Vlaggen*

France/Frankreich/Frankrijk

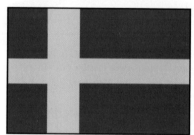
Poland/Polen

Australia/Australien/Australië

Germany/Deutschland/Duitsland

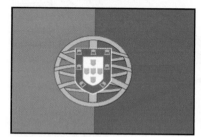
Portugal

Belgium/Belgien/België

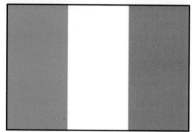
Ireland/Republik Irland/Ierland

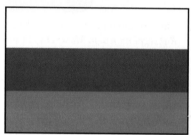
Russia/Rußland/Rusland

Belize

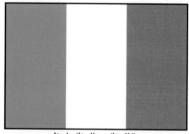
Italy/Italien/Italië

Scotland/Schottland/Schotland

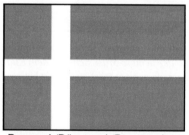
Denmark/Dänemark/Denemarken

Latvia//Lettland

Sweden/Schweden/Zweden

Estonia/Estland/Estonië

Netherland/Niederlande/Nederland

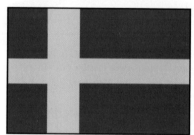
Ukraine/Ukraine/Oekraïne

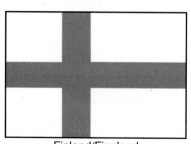
Finland/Finnland

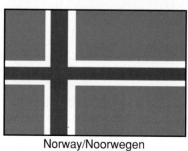
Norway/Noorwegen

U.K./Großbritannien/Verenigd Koninkrijk

Sails of a Tall Ship

Die Segel eines Großseglers

De zeilen van een groot zeilschip

1. Flying Jib
2. Outer Jib
3. Inner Jib
4. Fore Staysail
5. Fore Course
6. Fore Lower Topsail
7. Fore Upper Topsail
8. Fore Lower Topgallant
9. Fore Upper Topgallant.
10 Fore Royal
11. Main Staysail
12. Main Topmast Staysail
13. Main Topgallant Staysail
14. Main Course
15. Main Lower Topsail
16. Main Upper Topsail
17. Main Lower Topgallant
18 Main Upper Topgallant
19. Main Royal
20. Mizzen Staysail
21. Mizzen Topmast Staysail
22.Mizzen Topgallant Staysail
23. Crossjack
24. Mizzen Lower Topsail
25. Mizzen Upper Topsail
26. Mizzen Lower Topgallant.
27. Mizzen Upper Topgallant.
28. Mizzen Royal
29. Jigger Staysail
30. Jigger Topmast Staysail
31 Jigger Topgallant Staysail
32. Spanker
33. Spanker Topsail
34. Bowsprit
35. Foremast
36. Fore topmast
37 Fore Topgallant
38. Fore Royal Mast
39 Fore Royal Mast
40. Mainmast
41 Main Topmast
42 Main Topgallantmast
43 Main Royal Mast
44. Mizzenmast
45. Mizzen Topmast
46. Mizzen Topgallantmast
47. Mizzen Royal
48. Jigger Mast
49 Jigger Topmast
50 Spanker Boom
51 Spanker Gaff

1. Außenklüver
2. Klüver
3. Binnenklüver
4. Vorstengestagsegel
5. Focksegel
6. Voruntertopsegel
7. Vorobertopsegel
8. Vorunterbramsegel
9. Vorobербramsegel
10. Vorroyal
11. Großstagsegel
12. Großstengestagsegel
13. Großbramstagsegel
14. Großsegel
15. Großuntertopsegel
16. Großobertopsegel
17. Großunterbramsegel
18. Großoberbramsegel
19. Großroyal
20. Kreuzstagsegel
21. Kreuzstengestagsegel
22. Kreuzbramstagsegel
23. Achtersegel
24. Kreuzuntermarssegel
25. Kreuzobermarssegel
26. Kreuzunterbramsegel
27. Kreuzoberbramsegel
28. Kreuzroyal
29. Kreuzstagsegel
30. Kreuzstengestagsegel
31. Besan-Bramstagsegel
32. Besan
33. Besan-Topsegel
34. Bugspriet
35. Fockmast
36. Vormarsstenge
37. Vorbramstenge
38. Vorroyalstenge
40. Großmast
41. Großmarsstenge
42. Großbramstenge
43. Großroyalstenge
44. Besan-Mast
45. Besan-Marsstenge
46. Besan-Bramstenge
47. Kreuzroyal
48. Kreuzmast
49. Kreuzstenge
50. Besan-Baum
51. Besan-Gaffel

1. Grootstagzeil
2. Kluiver
3. Binnenkluiver
4. Voorstengstagzeil
5. Fok
6. Voorondertopzeil
7. Voorboventopzeil
8. Vooronderbramzeil
9. Voorbovenbramzeil
10. Voorbovenbramzeil
11. Stagfok
12. Grootstengstagzeil
13. Grootbramstagzeil
14. Grootzeil
15. Grootondertopzeil
16. Grootboventopzeil
17. Grootonderbramzeil
18. Grootbovenbramzeil
19. Grootbovenbramzeil
20. Bezaansstagzeil
21. Kruisstengstagzeil
22. Kruisbramstagzeil
23. Achterzeil
24. Kruisondermarszeil
25. Kruisbovenmarszeil
26. Kruisonderbramzeil
27. Kruisbovenbramzeil
28. Bezaanstopzeil
29. Bezaansstagzeil
30. Kruisstengstagzeil
31. Bezaansbramstagzeil
32. Bezaan
33. Bezaanstopzeil
34. Boegspriet
35. Fokkemast
36. Voormarssteng
37. Voorbramsteng
38. Voorbovenbramsteng
40. Grootmast
41. Grootmarssteng
42. Grootbramsteng
43. Grootbovenbramsteng
44. Bezaansmast
45. Bezaansmarssteng
46. Bezaansbramsteng
47. Bezaanstopzeil
48. Kruismast
49. Kruissteng
50. Bezaansboom
51. Bezaansgaffel

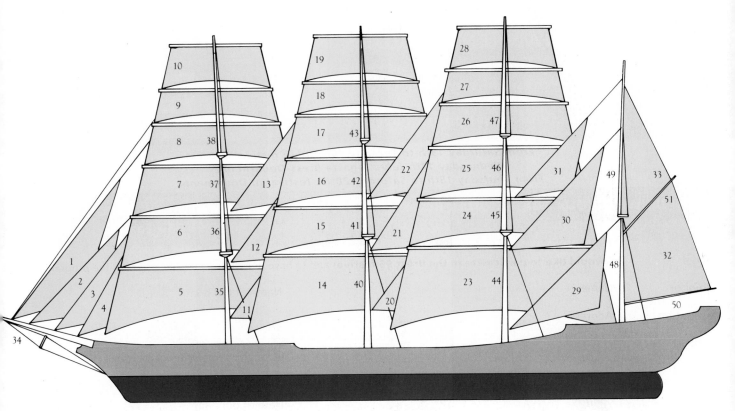

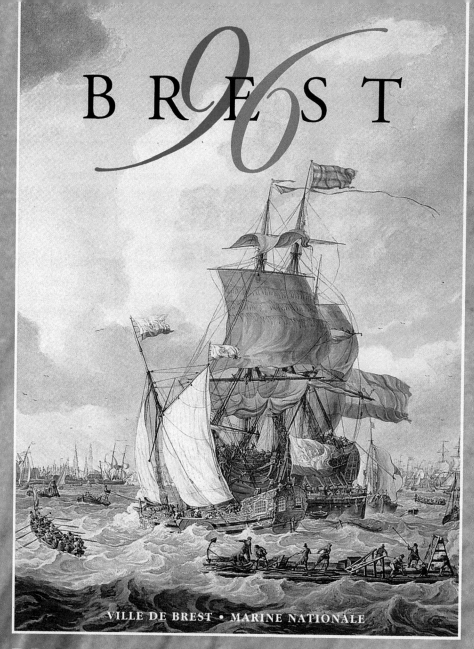

VILLE DE BREST • MARINE NATIONALE

BREST 96 : JULY, 13TH / 20TH 1996

INTERNATIONAL RENDEZ-VOUS FOR BOATS AND MARINERS

2 000 sailing boats manoeuvring in one of the most beautiful bays in the world • Hundre
of concerts, shows, exhibitions and entertainment ashore • 30 nations represented • A
exciting encounter with maritime culture and heritage • An engoing festival afloat and ash
re • A warm, genuine and cosmopolitan atmosphere •

From Saturday 13th to Tuesday 16th July : festival in Brest
Wednesday 17th July : regatta Brest-Douarnenez
From Thursday 18th to Saturday 20th : festival in Douarnenez

JOIN US WITH YOUR TRADITIONAL BOAT OR SHIP. EARLY REGISTRATION IS RECOMMENDED
Please, return to : **Brest 96 • BP 1996 • 29269 Brest Cedex • Tel. (33) 98 00 96 96 • Fax (33) 98 00 96 90**

☐ Owner   **I would like to participate in the Brest 96 festival** and to have more information concerning the programme

☐ Exhibitor   Name   Name of the boat

☐ Association   Address

☐ Modelist   Type

☐ Shipyard   Code   Town

☐ Musician   Country   Date of building

☐ Journalist   Phone   Length

FINE ART PRINTS ON THE TALL SHIPS

ABOVE, this superb Fine Art print visualises the Start of the **1995** Cutty Sark Tall Ships' Race. Printed on 135 gsm art paper, it shows the start of this year's series, when the Ships leave Edinburgh's Port of Leith and proceed towards the Forth's proud bridges, turn there and parade down river to the start of the race near the river's mouth. The QE2 cruise liner will be at the turning point, and we show Scotland's Malcolm Miller near her, with other Tall Ships in the background. The size is approx 16.5 by 23.4 inches.

There are two other companion prints. The first shows the Finish of the Columbus Race in **1992** at Liverpool, with the Sedov, Dar Mlodziezy, Kruzenshtern (all in this year's race), together with Mir (which will be at Bremerhaven). Sizes approx 20 by 27 inches (17 by 25 inches image size)

The third print shows the fleet leaving Newcastle for the start of the **1993** race, with Sedov and Dar Mlodziezy leaving the city for the starting line. Size approx 20 by 27 inches (17 by 25 inches image size)

We offer prints at £9.95 (95DKK/500BF/24DM/27Hfl) each, plus £3.00(30DKK/150BF/7DNM/8Hfl) post and packaging.

- -

I would like to buy _____ **of the 1995 print** _____ **of the 1993 print** _____ **of the 1992 print**

My name _____

My address _____

_____

I would like to buy ....copies of Tall Ships and the Cutty Sark Races by Paul Bishop, at the special price of £15.00/36DM/40Hfl/140DKK/750BF plus £3.00/7DM/8Hfl/30DKK/150BF post and packaging. I understand that I may return the book in good condition within a fortnight and claim back the £15.00/35DM/40Hfl.

My name ....

My address..

....

....

Cheques please to Churbarry Enterprises Ltd, 7 Craven Hill, London W2 3EN, England.

TALL SHIPS
AND THE
CUTTY SARK
RACES
PAUL
BISHOP

Michael Burnett
SPECIALIST TRADITIONAL YACHT BROKER

The Old Barn, Swanwick Shore Road,
Lower Swanwick, Nr Southampton, Hants SO31 7EF, ENGLAND.
Tel: (01489) 579 513   Fax: (01489) 589 052

FOR SALE

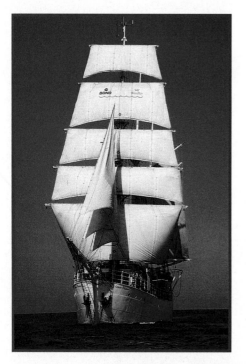

AMORINA

BARQUENTINE, BUILT
1934 STOCKHOLM,
CONVERTED FROM
LIGHTSHIP.
LOA 48.5M (159 FT)
LOD 35.0M (115 FT)
BEAM 7.7M (25 FT)
DRAFT 4.2M (14 FT)
SLEEPS 50
PLUS 10-14 CREW.
BASED EGYPT.
OWNER WILL SELL AS IS
OR HALF SHARE.

ZAMOURA

BARQUENTINE, BUILT HAMBURG 1927 AS A LUXURY YACHT FOR THE GERMAN KRUPP FAMILY. LOA 44M, LOD 36M, BEAM 7 M, DRAFT 2.9M. VERY NICE LINES AND COMING TO END OF LONG RENOVATION. ACCOMODATION IN LUXURY FOR 12 GUESTS AND 8-9 CREW.

ABOVE ARE TWO FROM OUR WIDE SELECTION OF CLASSIC YACHTS AND TRADITIONAL SHIPS, FROM 9.4M (31FT) TO 50M (165 FT). PLEASE CONTACT US WITH YOUR REQUIREMENTS WHETHER BUYING OR SELLING. WE ARE THE EXPERTS IN TRADITIONAL AND CLASSIC YACHTS.

The STA Schooners

Every year around 1,300 young men and women enjoy a once in a life time experience
They join as crew of one of two 150 foot Schooners called the Sir Winston Churchill and the Malcolm Miller and help sail these graceful romantic vessels for an unforgettable two weeks.

The youngsters concerned are not seasoned sailors - but during their voyage they will normally visit at least one foreign port and sail up to 1200 miles.

Birth of a dream

Thirty years ago, a retired London solicitor, Bernard Morgan, cherished a dream of bringing together the world's great sailing ships in a race.

In association with Commander Peter Godwin he put together a proposition which was eventually presented to Earl Mounbatten, then First Sea Lord. Mountbatten was immediately enthused by the idea, and enlisted the help of Captain Illingworth, a world expert on off-shore racing. As a result, in 1954 John Illingworth formed a committee to organise the first ever Tall Ships Race. It's success was so spectacular that the Sail Training Association (STA) was formed to guarantee the race's continuation as an annual event.

In the 1960's the STA decided to build a large ship of their own. Funds raised by public subscription led to the construction in 1966 of the Sir Winston Churchill, a three-masted topsail schooner. Two years later, the Malcolm Miller joined the fleet funded largely by Sir James Miller of Edinburgh in memory of his son.

Since those early beginnings, the two schooners have taken over 30,000 young people to sea giving them an unforgettable experience of the trials and triumphs of life aboard a tall ship

Adventures on the high seas

If you've never sailed a schooner, you'll probably be wondering what life on board a Tall Ship is really like. Those who have will confirm that it's certainly no cruise! Equally though, it's not unmitigated hardship. For some it's the kind of experience that looks better in hindsight, whilst others take immediately to the challenges of working in teams and the camaraderie that every ship engenders.

Each 39 strong crew is divided into three watches of 13. Each watch member helps care for and maintain the ship and takes part in watch duties like look-out , steering, sail trimming and assisting the cook in the galley.

The majority of the time is spent either on the bridge - perhaps taking the helm or keeping the ship's log - working on deck or aloft.

One of the most stimulating things about life at sea is the sheer unpredictability of the vast might of the ocean. At any moment all hands may be needed on deck in response to a gale. Alternatively, a calm day will bring the chance to relax and reflect.

Everyone on board an STA Schooner is reassuringly under the expert guidance of a carefully selected permanent crew. This consists of a Master, Chief Officer, Bosun, Engineer and Cook, along with a voluntary Afterguard comprising a qualified Navigator, three experienced Watch Officers, a Purser and an Assistant (Supernumerary).

Together, this team helps every crew member make the most of the experience and, of course, ensure the safety and will-being of their charges.

Despite the challenge of life on board, many participants are pleasantly surprised to find that there are some luxuries the STA considers essential - including central heating and high standard of amenities. All the STA's past crew members will testify to the enormous benefits they have gained in teamwork, in self-discipline, in leadership and decision-making skills.

For young people, the development of these strengths is obviously an excellent preparation for later life. But it's not just the 16-24 year old's age group that can learn from the experience. Recognising this, the STA operates Management Training voyages as an invaluable way of developing executive skills.

It is also possible to join one of the STA trips as a private individual.

Mixed sex voyages for the 24-29 year old age group are now regularly undertaken.

Although the STA is run along the lines of a normal business, it is in fact a registered charity with HRH the Prince Philip as its Patron.

It has always been the STA's ambition to bring the benefits of Sail Training to the widest possible number of people - especially those who would not normally be able to afford the kind of opportunities it offers.

The STA continuously raises money to maintain the ships - from donations, covenants and berth endowments. The supporters of the Association work tirelessly to raise these funds with the result that currently about 25 per cent of the true cost of each berth is subsidised.

It's worth remembering as you watch these majestic ships that they owe their existence to the thousands of people who have given both time and money so generously over the years. Without them, Bernard Morgan's dream would still be on the drawing board.

If you'd like to know more about sailing on the Sir Winston Churchill or the Malcolm Miller, either as a private individual or as a company, please contact the Sail Training Association, 2A The Hard, Portsmouth, Hampshire PO1 3PT, Telephone: 01705 832055, Fax 01705 815769.

If you are interested in supporting the STA or sponsoring a youngster on one of the voyages, the Chief Executive will be delighted to hear from you.

THE SAIL TRAINING ASSOCIATION
(A Company Limited by Guarantee and not for Profit)

Patron
His Royal Highness the Prince Philip Duke of Edinburgh, KG

Vice Patrons

INTERNATIONAL SAIL TRAINING ASSOCIATION

Chairman of the Racing Committee
Vice Admiral Sir George Vallings, KCB

Vice Chairman of the Racing Committee
Brigadier P R Duchesne, OBE

Racing Committee

Race Director
Lieutenant Colonel Peter J Newell

Race Director's Team
Lieutenant Commander Ian M Geraghty - Assistant Race Director
Janet E. Gauntlett - Secretary

Cutty Sark Scots Whisky Public Relations Manager
Amanda Suckling

Race Press Officer
Peter Smales

INTERNATIONAL ADVISORY COMMITEE
National Representatives of:

ISTA Race Headquarters, 5 Mumby Road, Gosport, Hants PO12 1AA   Tel: (01705) 586367 Fax: (01705) 584661

THE CUTTY SARK TROPHY

"Prized above all others"

The Cutty Sark Races bring together young people from around the world to race at sea in friendly competition and their principle objective is to encourage international understanding amongst these young crews.

The most important award in the Cutty Sark Tall Ships' Races is the one which is not actually raced for - the Cutty Sark Trophy. The winner attains tremendous prestige among the fleet.

The winners of the Cutty Sark Trophy are the crew and vessel which have contributed the most to international understanding and friendship during each annual series of races. It could go to any ship, large or small, and to any nationality, Russian, Polish, Swedish or British - any participating vessel can win the Cutty Sark Trophy.

The race organisers, the International Sail Training Association, do not decide who should win this special trophy, nor does the sponsor, Cutty Sark Scots Whisky, even though they present the award. The winner is decided by the votes of the captains of all the vessels in the race fleet. As the captains consult their crews on their choice, it can be said that the winners of the Cutty Sark Trophy have been chosen by all crews taking part.

The trophy itself is a valuable solid silver model of the "Cutty Sark" clipper which is one of the greatest 'tall ships' in history.

Captain & Crew of "Marineda", Spain, receiving the Trophy from Cutty Sark Scots Whisky's Managing Director Tony Easter in 1994.

Past winners of the Cutty Sark Trophy include:

"Kruzenshtern"	- Russia
"Zenobe Gramme"	- Belgium
"Gladan"	- Sweden
"Dar Pomorza"	- Poland
"Urania"	- Netherlands
"Sir Winston Churchill"	- UK
"Atlantica Av Gothenburg"	- Sweden
"Iskra"	- Poland
"Colin Archer"	- Norway
"Jens Krogh"	- Denmark
"Asgard II"	- Ireland
"Marineda"	- Spain

CUTTY SARK SCOTS WHISKY

Sponsor of the Cutty Sark Tall Ships' Races for over Twenty years

The Cutty Sark Tall Ships' Races are named after their sponsor - Cutty Sark Scots Whisky which, in turn, is named after one of the most famous tall ships of them all: the 19th Century Scottish clipper which is now in dry dock at Greenwich, London.

Cutty Sark Scots Whisky was named, in 1923, during a lunch at Berry Bros., the London based wine and spirit merchants. The partners were entertaining a well-known Scottish artist, James McBey. The conversation centered on a possible name for the pale coloured whisky which Berry Bros. was planning to sell to America. McBey suggested that the whisky should be called "Cutty Sark", after the ship which was in the news at that time. The clipper had just been brought back to English waters from Portugal, by Captain Dowman, a Cornish master mariner, who had seen her outrace a steamship in 1894.

The partners of Berry Bros.

were happy with this suggestion and asked McBey to design the label, featuring a sketch of the Cutty Sark clipper which remains unchanged to this day. Cutty Sark Scots Whisky has become as internationally renowned as its namesake and is one of the world's top selling Scotch whiskies, sold in over 120 countries.

Cutty Sark Whisky

strengthened its links with ships and sailing in 1972, when Berry Bros. & Rudd came to the rescue of the Sail Training Association (STA). The STA approached them for funds to help keep the annual tall ships' races afloat.

Once more, the joint topics of tall ships and whisky were discussed at the firm's historic premises. The conversation revolved around the growth of the races, since 1956, and how they continued to engender a spirit of friendly rivalry amongst the crews who compete from all round the world.

Over the past twenty years, Cutty Sark has been closely involved with the growth and development of the Cutty Sark Tall Ships' Races. Cutty Sark is delighted that, with support, the races are a continue to grow. The Sark Races now attr thousands of young from countries w ing political vie engage in frie at sea and m friendships

When you go aboard a large ship you can have her Official Stamp placed here.

Wenn Sie an Bord eines Windjammers gehen, können Sie den offiziellen Bordstempel erhaltern, den Sie hier plazieren.

Aan boord van de Tall Ships kunt u de officiële stempel van het schip krÿgen en hieronder laten plaatsen.

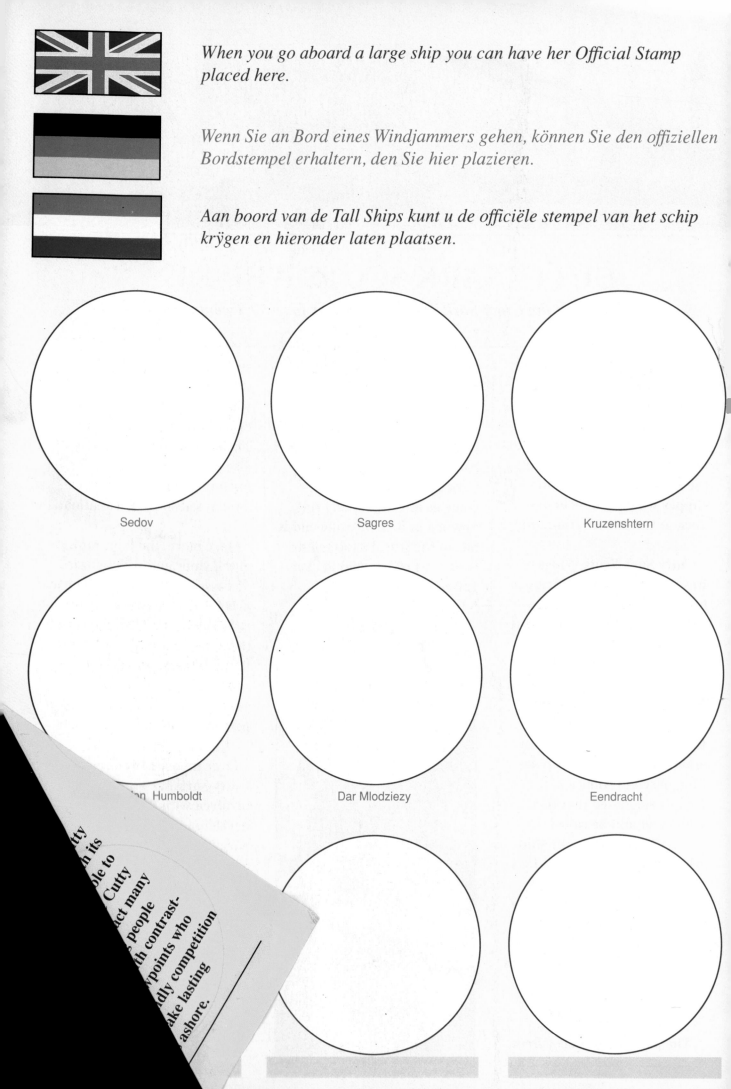

Sedov

Sagres

Kruzenshtern

Humboldt

Dar Mlodziezy

Eendracht